Pat,

Live life to the fullest and with no Regrets

Alfred Dempsey

TRIUMPH OF AN AMERICAN BLACK MAN

MY OWN STORY

BY
ALFRED DOUGLAS TURNIPSEED

iUniverse, Inc.
New York   Bloomington

Triumph of An American Black Man
My Own Story

Copyright © 2008 by Alfred Turnipseed

All rights reserved. No part of this book may be used or reproduced by any means, graphic, electronic, or mechanical, including photocopying, recording, taping or by any information storage retrieval system without the written permission of the publisher except in the case of brief quotations embodied in critical articles and reviews.

iUniverse books may be ordered through booksellers or by contacting:

iUniverse
1663 Liberty Drive
Bloomington, IN 47403
www.iuniverse.com
1-800-Authors (1-800-288-4677)

Because of the dynamic nature of the Internet, any Web addresses or links contained in this book may have changed since publication and may no longer be valid. The views expressed in this work are solely those of the author and do not necessarily reflect the views of the publisher, and the publisher hereby disclaims any responsibility for them.

ISBN: 978-0-595-48920-6 (pbk)
ISBN: 978-0-595-60895-9 (ebk)
ISBN: 978-0-595-49623-5 (cloth)

Printed in the United States of America

CONTENTS

Prologue — 1

The Early Years — 5
    Dramatic Life Change - Magnolia Tree - Dreaming

The Family — 15
Father - Mother - Other Family Members - Pinching My Brother - The Syrup Mill and Harvey's Fingers - Hanged

Adolescence And High School — 32
First Year - A Great Tragedy - The White Boy - High School, Second Year - Singing Debut, Doo Wop Group - Beaten up By Henry Rogers - High School, Third Year - Cha Cha Champion, Mauddy Bee's - High School, Senior Year - Graduation

The College Years — 62
Freshman Year - A College Major and A Rude Awakening - Sophomore Year - Dr. Killingsworth, Mr. Wayman Carver - The Chinese Opera

The Magnificent Group — 75
Eula V. Arnold - Clifford and Everlyn Turnipseed - M. T. Starr - Barbara Welborn - Pal Harris - Rev. C. L. Henderson

Out On My Own — 82
    Racism

A New Beginning — 86
    Junior Year - Stuttering - Edna Freeman

Senior Year — 94
    Requirements - Graduation

Post Graduation — 97
    New York - Hazel Bryant - Marie Alder

The United States Army — 101
    Assignment Change - Chaplain's Assistant - Asian Experiences

Army, Stateside 113
    Promotion - Bob Guess - A Life Changing Challenge - Rebirth

Triumph 124

Epilogue 127

DEDICATION

Before I began this book, several questions ran through my mind: What would be my purpose for writing it, and to whom would I address? Many months, weeks, and hours were spent pondering those very questions. But after wading through these thoughts, I realized there was a need to complete this project for myself. A written record of my early life and struggles needed to be documented. I also wanted to share these experiences with my immediate family as a written witness to my life before they knew me. But thinking more about this project, I decided to share it with others. Therefore this is an unburdening, a cleansing of my soul, a sharing of my thoughts and experiences. Maybe the unfolding of my life, especially the difficult periods, will be motivational and inspirational to young people having difficulty at trying to find their way in the world. This book is dedicated to those very purposes.

This book is also dedicated to the American family. In the most difficult years of my early life, the great stabilizing force was my family. They sustained and nurtured me and were most instrumental in my development.

But in recent years, the family has been downgraded in many circles, to a second class institution. But without my family, it would have been very difficult for me to survive.

In my dedication to the family, I would like this institution once again, to reclaim its lofty heights. This is necessary, if the world is going to be a better place for all of us to live.

ACKNOWLEDGMENTS

I would like to thank posthumously, these great people.

Miss Eula Arnold, my savior, mentor, and friend.

Barbara Welborn, my loving sister, role model, and friend.

Clifford Turnipseed, my father, protector, and friend

Rev. C.L. Henderson, my supporter, and good friend

Pal Harris, my supporter, and good friend

I would also like to thank the living members of this magnificent group. They include Everlyn Turnipseed, M.T and Catherine Starr. Without your support, this book wouldn't have been written. And without your help, the quality of life I enjoy today wouldn't have been possible.

Thanks to the community of Jonesboro for hanging in there with me, when times were difficult.

PROLOGUE

My family **was** very poor. We lived in a shanty type house with four rooms. Five siblings shared one bedroom with two beds. All of our food came from my grandfather's farm. And there were no inside plumbing or bathroom facilities. I didn't have many clothes, but ma kept them very clean and neat. But what I did have was plenty of love and great emotional support. Being poor wasn't the major issue in my life, not being able to communicate was the most compelling problem. I had a very bad speech impediment. So my life was filled with much pain and many setbacks. Therefore the love of my family was paramount while facing the challenges of the future.

All during my growing up years, I worked to help support myself. I could find the most creative ways of making money. Fixing bicycle chains, painting car tires, caddying, selling copper, feeding chickens, picking blackberries, mowing lawns, and digging septic tank holes, were a few of the odd jobs I had. With some of the money earned, I would on occasion treat myself to a big ice cream soda.

My speech impediment was stuttering. Because of this, I was ostracized, bullied, and was the butt of many jokes. This would be my lifelong battle. Stuttering relegated me at a very young age, to a life of loneliness and despair. My family was always on hand with their support of me. And in my situation, I needed it. But somehow I believed that my situation would change in the future. I just had to endure and to persevere. I battled being isolated and lonely all during my early years. For a young man in the formative years of his life, socialization was tremendously important. My thoughts, ideas, and feelings, couldn't be shared with a good friend, because I had none. I would sometimes lie under this huge magnolia tree and have a conversation with myself. This would relieve some of the tension of being a social misfit. Lying on the ground, looking up into the sky, watching birds fly overhead, was also a very peaceful experience. This became a regular routine. But I cried sometimes because no one was there to hear me.

I always wondered why God did this to me. My very existence was questioned many times. Why was I saddled with such a burden? Was I cursed? And I was a really good kid.

As I would learn later, these experiences helped to shape my life and made me mentally stronger. I told myself for the next twenty years, things would someday change for the better. So I prayed to God for help, to endure until the change could come.

While in high school, my social life was practically non-existent. Being a stutterer, I had difficulty communicating. Boys didn't want to interact with me and girls shunned me. But they ridiculed me at every opportunity. I was called a non-talking M--F-- on many occasions. I walked to school alone, ate lunch alone, and watched the other children play. I waited for my turn that never came. So I learned to exist alone. Since there was nothing I could do and with no where to turn, I was sad and retreated farther into myself.

I lived in a cocoon. Why wouldn't I just end it as some teenagers of today might do and commit suicide. Of course I thought about this, but never considered it a serious option.

I simply held onto the belief that this curse would someday be lifted. Sure I was depressed, but never to the point where my cup runneth over.

In today's world, with all of its technology and all of its promise, there is still a lack of hope among many young people. The promise of a better life is a fleeting dream. Young people talk about the lack of opportunity. I have heard the cries and laments of these young people. I say to them, hang in there, persevere, and become more prepared to meet the challenges of the world.

Living in a ghetto, being part of an underprivileged group, having a disadvantaged background, inner-city kids, are terms used by social scientists and by society to define African Americans living on the down side of middle class. I have lived through it all and it is possible to survive.

Society has placed in the path of success for a segment of the population, many, many, obstacles designed to destroy, dishonor, demean, and discourage. Many young Black Americans have bought into this thinking pattern. As a result of this brain washing, Black America's self esteem has suffered. Lack of quality education, jobs and housing are just a few of these obstacles. There are others. And this is all part of racism.

My self esteem suffered for other reasons. I had a two parent home, loving brothers and sisters, a good family situation. And I was poor. Most of the families around me were also poor. But this was not banged over my head by over zealous social scientists. I couldn't communicate with others. This was my greatest obstacles.

With my stuttering, lack of acceptable communication skills, and problems with educational opportunities, my self esteem was at an all time low. I didn't like myself. I wasn't worth anything and had no real future. Since I couldn't communicate, I was perceived to be dumb. This is how my peers and acquaintances had defined me. If you are told something negative about yourself enough times, and it is constantly drummed in your head, you will begin to believe it. Part of me believed what my peers said.

On top of this, I was afraid to take even the tiniest risk for fear of failure. That is what low self esteem will do. The fear of failure will defeat most of us. Actually, it is the fear of success. Being a failure, you certainly know how to fail. But to go into the unknown and try and make a change is frightening. Being fearful of this unknown, namely success, keeps you in the world of failure. You must learn to crash out. In trying, you may fail. But not taking a risk at all will guarantee failure. I have learned what people think of you doesn't have to become your reality. You must find a way to change the perception of yourself, thereby creating a more positive image. You must learn to like yourself.

Prologue

Don't be defined by your financial success or the lack of it, or the community you live in, your race, creed, or your gender. Be defined by your spirit, your soul, and your character. Armed with this new positive image, your chances improve greatly. Believe the change is possible and make it happen.

But with my problems relating from not being able to communicate, it was very difficult to think positively. My emotions were in constant conflict. I suffered greatly, had bouts of depression, and fought many demons while waiting for the change to come.

I didn't lose hope, because hope was all I had. I just prayed that God would hear me. This was my daily supplication for the next twenty years. The change had to come.

Ma told me that most of us have conflicts with our emotions. And I was not depressed and sad all the time. There were flashes of great joy, especially during athletic events. I was a good athlete and didn't have to depend on my speaking voice when engaged in athletic activity. Many family events also gave me great joy.

One was defeating my older sister in a bicycle race. She was the king of the hill. So we had a great race. I remember preparing for this event. I exercised my body, serviced my bicycle, and my mind was turned to this every race. This was a big deal to me. My sister was tough. The day of the race was full of excitement. Our peers and family members were there. It began, and we were nip and tuck for most of the race. It lasted for about a mile, and was very physically draining. Finally, I prevailed. I had won!! I won!! My sister was the first to congratulate me. She gave me a big hug. And our bonding grew stronger because she was such a good sport. Other family members and peers were elated. With mini triumphs and victories like this, I was able to laugh and to feel really happy during these times. I was able to forget the unremitting affliction that gripped me.

THE EARLY YEARS

I was born in a small Atlanta suburb named Jonesboro Georgia. It is located about five miles south of the Atlanta Airport. There were seven brothers and sisters including myself. I was fourth from the bottom and the top.

My parents were unskilled laborers, and we were extremely poor. But we were rich in love and caring. My father went only to the third grade in school. Mother had an eighth grade education. And they worked very hard to provide for the family.

In rural black families, education for the children ended at the eighth grade level in many southern communities. The reason was, to help their parents support the family. This was encouraged by rural white America. While working with my father on the junk truck, I heard a white man ask him. "Why don't you take that boy out of school so he can help you and the family full time?" "What does he need an education for?" My father didn't reply. But some black families did take their children out of school for that very reason. Black families that stressed education in the presence of whites were considered dangerous and uppity by the rural white community. And blacks risked losing their jobs or even physical harm. This was well known in the black communities. And this type of conversation was commonplace.

At the same time, the white family's children were encouraged to finish high school and even go to college. This was also common knowledge in rural black southern America. This was the practice.

This way of thinking never did set right in my mind. This was my first head on collision with racism and who controlled the society in which we lived. Since most black people in the south were less educated than whites, encouraging blacks to quit school was the way white society made sure that the status quo remained.

But my earliest recollection of anything, or any event, was going with my father to Atlanta to purchase a 1936 Chevrolet. This must have been about 1950 because I was a very young boy and my father held me in his arms. Going down into a field where the grass was very tall, there was this old green Chevy. My father sat me on the front seat and started the engine. The car was kind of dirty and I didn't like it very much. But father drove off in this car with my sister and me in the back seat, to our home in Jonesboro. This was a very significant event because it was our first car, at least the first one I knew about.

From this point on, my father's car-buying patterns had been established. He purchased cars that were ten to fifteen years old. This would continue throughout his life.

I don't remember too much for the next two or three years, except when it was time to go to school. Well actually, I didn't go to school at this point, because I was too young. My sisters had to baby-sit for me. Therefore they took me to school with them, to a one-room schoolhouse. Imagine a one-room schoolhouse. It is a school like on the T. V. show, "Little House on the Prairie." All classes were housed in one room. It is difficult to believe there were one-room schools in the late fifties, in the city of Atlanta. Well Jonesboro was an Atlanta suburb.

I don't remember the first or the second grades. I suspect one or both were skipped. This would account for me graduating much earlier than my peers. Since I had gone to school with my sisters, the teachers thought earlier materials had been mastered. I did go to the third grade, but without much memory of it.

I do remember the fourth grade. My school was in Clayton County, which is within the city of Jonesboro. An issue arose concerning the water system of this County. All fourth grades students had to write an essay on the water system bond issue. I don't know why. But all fourth grade children had to participate.

My essay was judged third best in the county. I don't know whether it was third best among colored and white schools, or just colored schools. All schools in the South were segregated. But receiving the third place prize was a very special moment in my life. The colored school, my family, and friends, were all very proud of me. The care free life in the fourth grade, along with good teachers, made life very simple but happy, at this point.

My life took a dramatic change in the fifth grade. A major event turned my world upside down. And life as I had known it up to now, was gone in a matter of minutes.

I was given one of the lead roles in a school play. Since I had lead roles in other plays before, the teacher arbitrarily assigned this part to me. But I didn't like the role.

I was to play an Indian who was portrayed as uncivilized and unintelligent. I felt that this role had negative connotations, and it just didn't feel right to me. So I voiced my opinion over and over as to why I didn't want this role. As a black boy, I identified with Indians and their plight. Even at this young age, I understood racism and exploitation. This was a very sensitive issue and I felt uncomfortable being a part of it. America in my opinion had not treated Indians very well. So over my strong objections, and after listening to my reasons, the teacher ordered me to play the role. Since the teacher's word was law, I had to comply.

Rehearsals went very well, and I was having no problems with my lines. But I continued to have a strange feeling of impending doom lurking ahead, in the pit of my stomach. And on assembly day, the whole school filed into the auditorium to see the play. Excitement and anticipation were everywhere. The children were restless. The teachers were nervous. This was supposed to be a good day. Now it was time for the play to begin.

The curtains opened slowly. And here I was, a very small boy standing in the middle of this huge stage. My costume was a paper

Indian headdress. I had on overalls with high top shoes. There was a paper leather strip pinned up and down the legs of my overall pants.

I had large eyes and a cherubic face. Being such a little boy, the large stage really engulfed me.

The play started. And I stepped up to deliver my lines. To my shock and utter amazement, strange sounds began to come from my mouth. "All hail our White Brothers" is what I should have said. But it sounded like this. "A-a-a-a-a-a-a-all h-h-h-h-h-h-hail ou-ou-ou-our wh-wh-wh-wh-wh-white bro-bro-bro-bro-brothers". What was the matter with me? What happened to my voice? I was stuttering.

With their eyes wide open and staring directly at me, the student body was stunned and sat in stone silence for a few seconds. They thought I was joking. But when they realized I was serious, laughter began to fill the assembly hall. Nothing but hysterical chatter and giggling could be heard for the next few minutes. There was total chaos until order was restored. Then another player recited a few lines, and it was back to me for more dialogue. The student body continued to look at me not knowing what would happen next.

I-I-I-I-I-, every word I tried to deliver came out in a stutter. And the more I stuttered, the more the students laughed. There was so much noise in the assembly hall order couldn't be restored despite attempts to do so by the school's principal. After a while the play resumed, I again tried desperately to deliver my lines. Nothing came from my mouth that was understandable, just more stuttering like I-I-I-I-ar-ar-ar. I couldn't believe what was happening to me. Tears swelled up in my eyes, my lips trembled, my stomach ached, and my knees buckled, but I still tried to deliver my lines. All eyes were on me and I was completely overcome with fear.

At that moment, I just wanted to vanish and relieve myself of this pain and embarrassment.

Stripped of all pride and dignity, I felt naked in full view of the whole student body. By now, the laughter was deafening. It was loud, louder, and louder. The student body was now out of control. I felt even smaller than before, and just wanted to run away and hide....and die.

This whole episode lasted maybe ten minutes at the most, but it seemed like an eternity. It was clear to everyone listening that I couldn't continue. The stage curtains were drawn. The play was cancelled, but I couldn't move. My feet and body were frozen to the very spot where I was left standing before the curtains were drawn. My teacher, (Miss Thompson), realized this and came to assist me off the stage. She had to physically lift me since I couldn't move. And at that moment, I began to cry uncontrollably. Miss Thompson was also crying. She held me in her arms for a few moments while trying to console me, but to no avail. I was trembling all over. Then she apologized over and over. For the rest of the day, I was in a zombie like state, with no feelings or control over my body. Since I could not walk or talk, my teacher had to take me home. But I was the laughing stock of the whole school, and the kids were relentless in their ridicule of me. They teased and taunted me for the rest of my school career.

From that day on, whenever the teacher saw me and until her death, she apologized. She admitted that she had been wrong. It took a few years, but I forgave Miss Thompson for this incident. She became my good friend and a great supporter.

The fallout from this incident would remain with me forever. Never having any speech problems before, I became a stutterer and still am now. From being an outgoing, gregarious, and an extrovert, I became an introvert living inside myself. Afraid to speak to anyone, I lived in a cocoon for many years. I wrote notes to express my thoughts and ideas. This would become my mode of communication. This cocoon became my prison, but I couldn't have survived my pain and suffering living on the outside of it. My life had changed forever.

The rest of my elementary schools days were lived in a fog. I don't remember too much about them. My days of participation in school plays were over. I became an anonymous being, always in the background, and afraid of the world and fearful of any activity where speaking was involved.

The Early Years

To me, I had become less than a human being. I was always taught humans were social animals, and engaged in activities that would bind them together. Since I didn't think of myself capable of this interaction, in my eyes, I was outside the realm of being human and in a state of confusion. For many years, I thought of myself as less than human.

But among the last things I do remember about elementary school, were the May Day events. Each class would present some type of dance around a pole situated on the school campus. This was called the May-Pole. Parents, friends, and sometimes others schools joined in the activities of this day. Classes with their colorful costumes augmented the festival. These activities were performed outdoors. This was really great and I will always remember it as being very positive.

As a stutterer, I needed space to get away from the ridicule of my friends and neighbors. In my community, there were no schools, hospitals, or therapy for people with this type of impediment. None of the teachers or parents knew anything about this problem. So I suffered with it.

Living in the South gave me a great opportunity to visit my grandfather's farm. It was the hub of activity for his thirty children, their husbands, wives, children, and grandchildren. This farm was also an oasis for me. There was a large magnolia tree on the farm. It gave refuge from the many storms raging within me. It was located about one hundred yards south of the farmhouse. I would ride my bike there to lie under this huge magnolia and give myself pep talks. A great deal of time would be spent there over the next few years. It also did wonders for my psyche. Some of the things I told myself went something like this. You are a stutterer. This is the sum total of your life as far as your friends and neighbors are concerned. But they know nothing about your innermost feelings, what is in your heart, how you feel about your life, your family, or your aspirations. But I knew inside this stutterer's mind, was someone who needed love, understanding, and a sense of belonging. And I continually reminded myself, while lying under this tree, that a change would someday come.

This magnificent, magnanimous, and magical Magnolia Tree was my safety net. It gave me a place to unwind. Because this place was so special, I would revisit it many times to be regenerated. I didn't profess to be a very religious person at this point in my life, but this tree became very sacred to me with spiritual and religious overtones. It remains very special in my heart.

In the midst of all the confusion in my life, other skills were developing. I couldn't communicate verbally. So I communicated in non verbal ways. When one sense is lost, another is developed. My ability to listen, to feel, to touch, and to understand were all heightened.

One day at school, I was sitting on a big rock near the playground watching the other kids play. Since I had trouble speaking, the kids didn't include me in their play games. A girl named Bertie Allen came up to me and started talking. She was an outcast like me and wasn't included in the play games either. It didn't seem to matter to her whether I could speak or not. She just opened up to me. I didn't say a word, just listened. There was pain in her eyes and in her voice as she poured out her heart to me. I touched her slightly from time to time, on the hand, during the conversation. This gesture seemed to calm her when she became too excited as the conversation got particularly painful. When she finished, her eyes glistened and her face sparkled. She had the look of a person who had been relieved of a huge burden. Someone had listened. Someone had understood. Someone had cared.

This sort of thing happened, in various ways, many times in my life. People seem to sense that I would listen, comfort, and understand. If this happened during a period when I felt particularly worthless, it somehow made me feel worthy of someone with a special gift. And since I could become sensitive to the pain and suffering of others, this was now part of my new awareness.

Growing up, I had to work. Since my father was a junk man, I had to wake up in the morning about 3am. We would get dressed in ragged work clothes and go load the truck with junk until 9am. Then I was off to school. After school, it was back to work with my father, to load the junk truck again. About 7pm, we would finish.

My homework had to be completed before going to bed. Now this way of life was repeated about three times a week. After loading the truck and finishing about 9am, my father would take me to school in the junk truck. I would lie down on the floor so other children couldn't see me. But ultimately, they would see and tease me. It was certainly embarrassing to be call "junkman" by your peers. But it didn't seem to bother my father at all.

He didn't pay me for the many hours of work. To him, this was my duty. But every Saturday, he bought me a Sugar Daddy. This was a huge candy bar, and I was happy to get it. To me it wasn't about money at this point. The fact that father knew I like this candy and he was willing to make me feel happy and appreciated was all I needed. This became the highlight of my week. And I didn't feel underpaid.

Father for the most part, was pretty kind. He didn't abuse me and I liked being around him. But since I liked the fashions of the day, money had to be earned by working at various other jobs. But I continued to work very hard throughout my elementary and high school careers with my father.

Although I was a stutterer, the people of the community essentially liked me. They teased me, but I guess this was part of my growing up process. I lived with this problem and continued to pray that things would get better.

In the community, we participated in all type of sport activities. Boys and girls participated equally. We had bicycle races, foot races, baseball hitting contests, and I was always among the leaders. These small victories made my life somewhat bearable.

I had great athletic ability. But being so small, people took me for granted. Most of the boys and girls in my community couldn't defeat me in any of the sport activities. I had an eight-foot high basketball goal in my back yard. All kids in the neighborhood were invited to come over and play anytime.

I could make eight out of ten shots from anywhere on the court at anytime. In the language of the day, I was a killer on this basketball court. Well, they considered me the champ.

Armed with this, I went to the gymnasium. The standard height for a basketball goal is ten feet, and I never realized it. Trying to make baskets in the gymnasium was a disaster. After being able to make eight out of ten baskets in my back yard and one out of ten in the gymnasium, I realized that basketball wasn't my sport.

But the back yard meetings with the boys and girls in the community made my life, which I thought was unbearable at times, in fact, pleasant to some degree. But between the low points and the little victories, I was often very confused.

Growing older, I was becoming more aware of girls. But they made fun of me because I couldn't speak properly. Most words coming out of my mouth began with either A-a-a-a-a or Th-th-th. I talked to Ma about the opposite sex and she did her best to explain many things about girls to me. But she couldn't make contact with them for me.

Of course, this was not the only thing. The seemingly bottomless pit I had lived in for most of my life was growing deeper. How would the world know that I existed?

I used to dream, especially when alone, that I was standing on the top of this huge mountain crying out to the world below: "I am a person that is very much alive!!" I would pace back and fourth yelling and screaming at the world below from a perch on the mountain above. Please, please, notice me, hear me. The world would just continue to go about its normal activities.

Then one day, after much screaming, pleading, and praying, the world would pause, stop its activities and look up at me. Then with outstretched arms, the world would embrace me, love me, accept me, and tell me I was a member in good standing with the world. This would also mean that I was a real person...finally.

Throughout all the difficult periods of my life, I maintained a vivid imagination. I became a pretty creative kid, while searching for my true self.

I built a very elaborate tree house. I even built a three-hole golf course in my back yard. At that time, my family lived on six or seven acres of land. And this was quite a project. The course has sand traps, a water hazard, and several other obstructions to test my golfing skills. Maybe a golf course architect was in the making. But living in the segregated south, there was no chance. In the north, chances weren't good either, especially since there were no recognized black golf course architects at that time. Racism was also a big factor in the golf industry.

Doing all these things, I still questioned my existence; why was I here? So again I had the same lament, how does a boy who thinks he has nothing, become a relevant person?

THE FAMILY

To understand the type of person I was, my upbringing, my values, my spirit, my compassion, and my passion, it is necessary to meet my family. Without them, my development would have been dramatically altered. My family was very strong and very well respected in the community of Jonesboro.

Father

My father was named Clifford Turnipseed. I called him Da-Cliff without knowing the reason why. He was a stepfather who had come into my life at a very young age. Although learning about this was quite a shock, it really didn't matter. Da-Cliff is a short version for Daddy Cliff. I suppose mother started that name for me. Since I never felt like a stepchild, and he was the only father I ever knew, this was never an issue in my life. He was and will always be my father.

He was a man accustomed to very hard work. Formal education ended in the third grade for this self made man. He was reared with seven other boys. His father was named Spence and his mother was Viola. They were very strict disciplinarians. And I never knew them very well.

Da-Cliff was also fairly strict. He was a very strong willed man, very stubborn, and would not hesitate to impose his will on any family member. This is how he believed the head of a family should be. Men were considered to be the head of the family unit and Da-Cliff tried to exert this type of leadership. Many times we thought he was wrong. He thought he was right, so we couldn't and didn't dare question his authority. We believed he had our best interest at heart, well most of the time anyway.

He was about five feet, eleven inches tall. His muscles were quite large and he was very fit and trim. Looking at his muscles with admiration, physically I wanted to be just like him.

Most of the time, Da-Cliff was fair. I always had the impression that he cared for me. This gave me a measure of security. Although Da-Cliff could be extremely difficult sometimes, I don't want to give the impression that he was unkind, brutal, or abusive. But as a child growing up under his rule, I sincerely thought so at some point.

Da-Cliff worked most of the time. He had no hobbies other than going to church. Sitting on the porch of our house was his only form of relaxation. He didn't dance, play ball, or go to the movies.

In my very early life, Da-Cliff was employed at Delta Airlines. This job came to an early end when he had gotten ill. His job was to clean engine parts for the airplane mechanics. The chemicals used for this cleansing, made Da-Cliff extremely ill. Therefore his doctor advised him to give up the job. This decision probably saved his life because another brother later died from a blood disorder while doing the same job.

This decision changed the financial direction of the family from the security of Delta Airlines to the insecurity of being a junkman.

Since Da-Cliff had no education, I suppose he did the best thing possible. I am sure he thought so.

Da-Cliff always owned a truck. This was of course for junk. But sometime, he would place chairs in the back of the truck. This is where children rode whenever the family went visiting or to church. And this was actually fun. Ma and Da-Cliff rode up front in the cab section of the truck. And there was always a canvas in the back. If it rained, Da-Cliff would raise and stretch the canvas over the back portion of the truck to keep us dry. This was quite effective.

In many instances, Da-Cliff wasn't very enterprising. In the case of junk cars, he would buy them as a whole unit. The junkyard owners would pay more money if these cars were cut up in small pieces. So we used an axe and a sledgehammer to cut up these cars. Can you imagine the hard work used to accomplish this? It took us sometimes most of the day just for this purpose.

Had Da-Cliff been just a little more enterprising, he could've purchased a blowtorch to cut up the junk cars, and accomplish the same thing in a fraction of the time. We could've bought and sold more junk cars. But he wouldn't hear of this, so we did things his way.

But one of his more imaginative and enterprising ideas was this. Since we also sold wood for heaters and potbellied stoves, he built a saw mill in our back yard. Imagine having a saw mill in your yard. Let me describe this just a little bit more.

He would park his truck next to a pulley setup. The truck was jacked up on one side, usually the left side rear tire. Blocks were placed in front and behind the other tires. This kept the truck stable.

The gas pedal could now be depressed. The left rear jacked up tire would spin. But before this, a long belt was placed and stretched over the jacked up tire on one end. The other end was hooked up to the pulley. Attached to the pulley was a huge circular saw, with a kind of counter top that would move back and forth toward the saw. With the motor on in the truck, and the gas pedal depressed, this huge saw would spin. This was quite dangerous because the belt could break. I can remember this happening several times. To the outsider, this whole operation was frightening. Well it was dangerous and we had to really stay alert at all times.

A piece of wood called a slab was placed on the counter top. As it was pushed forward, the saw would cut it. Da-Cliff was usually the pusher. My sister was the feeder, the one to get the slabs. My job was to hold the slab being cut. I was within inches of this huge saw that could easily cut me to pieces.

My sister and I would sometimes exchange jobs. But Da-Cliff would never let us be the pusher because this was the most dangerous job in the whole operation. If he had slipped at anytime, he would've probably been cut to pieces. Well none of us were ever injured from this, but we all came very close.

We had to breathe lots of sawdust and were always aware that the belt on the pulley could break and decapitate us. But after doing this for a while, it became routine for all of us.

I often wonder whether Da-Cliff had a sense of humor. With the children, he did not. Parents in this poor community, who I knew, didn't get into laughing and playing with their children. I don't want to give the impression that Da-Cliff was a cold man, quite the contrary. Parents were the authority, and children listened and obeyed.

I didn't know anything about his innermost feelings, his dreams, or his aspirations. But in the rural south, parent's dreams were often wrapped up in their children. His job was to take care of his family and he did that to the best of his ability.

I enjoyed a pretty good relationship with Da-Cliff. And when I became an adult, the relationship grew stronger. But I still regret not knowing him better as a person, especially in my early years.

Mother

I could always count on my mother to be there in the time of need. I called her then and still call her Ma. Her childhood was extremely difficult. She was the product of a strong patriarchal father who was very restrictive. Ma's mother, my grandmother, died in 1931. So I never knew her. Grandfather then married a woman nineteen years of age, about one year later. Ma was seventeen at the time and grandfather was fifty years of age.

Ma often worked eight or ten hours a day. She was a domestic worker who also had her own family to look after. Somehow, she made it work. Her formal education had ended at the eighth grade level. She was a strong willed woman and was very independent. Growing up in a society where the man was considered to be in charge of the family unit, Ma held her own ground. She was the one who held us all together.

Ma defended her children when Da-Cliff was overzealous in his punishment. She defended us in the community when local bullies threatened. And Ma supported us when we had confrontations with emotional and social issues. I knew Ma loved me. She always made her feelings very clear. Growing up in my family, Ma never used the term, "I love you." But I suspect she didn't know how to say it, because she was not taught by her parents to use this phrase. But I always had the feeling of being loved. Ma would see that our clothes for school were clean, had a lunch, and that we had food to eat after arriving home from school, although she wasn't home.

Ma was a disciplinarian, but not like Da-Cliff. She handled all chore assignment like washing clothes, washing dishes, and sweeping the yards. And Ma was very good at assigning chores.

She took a couple of extended family members into our home. Her brother, George Gresham Sr., married a woman with a questionable reputation. To help ease the situation, Ma took George Jr. and his sister Gloria into our home. We were the poorest family in the neighborhood. But Ma insisted on taking them in and somehow it worked.

When we went to church, and we went every Sunday, Da-Cliff would sing. He sang very often and very loud, actually shouting sometimes. Ma was embarrassed by this and would just bow her head to get away from hearing Da-Cliff. He really couldn't sing, but was very good at trying.

At Christmas, each child hoped to receive one toy or gift. For the small children, it was of course Santa's job to bring gifts. All children in my family would find a shoebox to be used at this time. These shoeboxes would be placed under the Christmas tree. Hopefully Santa would fill these boxes with fruit. Well this was a tradition in our family. So every Christmas, Ma made sure that all of us had something under the tree. This made her very happy.

One Christmas, every boy about the age of thirteen [my age] in the neighborhood, received a new bicycle except me. I was very sad, although Ma had given me a gift. But when she found out, tears streamed down her cheeks. She promised that I would have a new bike by the next Christmas if it killed her.

After the New Year, Ma went to the local Western Auto Store and purchased me a red J C Higgins bicycle, on which she paid one dollar a week until it was paid for. Now the next Christmas, I was the envy of every boy in the neighborhood, when I sported a shiny new red bike. This was a very special Christmas because of the sacrifice Ma made for me. I was very touched by this gesture and the feeling of love for her is in my heart everyday. Ma was indeed a special person.

She didn't campaign for equal rights or anything close to that, but could do almost anything a man did .She would paint the house, fix the stove, fix the washing machine and much more. One day, Ma was painting the interior of our house. She instructed my sister and me to hold the ladder while she painted the ceiling. Somehow Ma slipped and fell. The paint ended up on her head and in her face.

My sister and I thought it was funny, so we laughed and laughed and laughed. Ma was angry and she whipped us for laughing. We now make jokes about how Ma fell into the paint bucket. She will staunchly deny this, but we tease her to this day

Remembering the many ways Ma showed her love, I am extremely proud and feel lucky to have her as my mom. She really taught me the meaning of family. We discussed our family tree many times. I learned about my grandparents, great grandparents, and great-great grandparents. Ma was a wealth of information about many things.

One topic we talked about was hate. And her exact words to me were, "don't get into that hate thing, it takes energy, and you must use your energy for something positive." All through my life up to now, I have lived by this philosophy. Over the past two decades, Ma and I have enjoyed an even better relationship.

Other family members

Aside from Ma and Da-Cliff, there were seven brothers and sisters. Ma actually gave birth to nine children. One sister died in childbirth. And another sister survived only to the age of one.

My eldest sister was named Ethel. We called her "Caliva." I didn't know her very well. Mainly because she had gotten married and moved away, by the time I was four years old.

Occasionally we would see each other, and always had an enjoyable visit. She later moved closer to the family home and I got to know her better. We had a great relationship from that point onward.

She introduced me to liquor in New York around the middle sixties. We went to a nightclub called "The Savoy" one evening. And I had about one tablespoon full of Vodka. Boy was I sick. That night I lost my virginity, but only to alcohol. Now that was a very memorable evening.

I purchased my first music album with help from Caliva. As we listened to this album called "Concert by The Sea" by Cal Tjader one day, the drummer on this album took a solo. She jumped to her feet, and in typical Caliva fashion, yelled "blow boy blow." I said, "Caliva, those are drums playing." She regained her senses and let go with a huge grin. This incident became a joke between the two of us. It was repeated many times after this day. And we continued to have a very good relationship.

Barbara is next. We called her Bobbie. She lived with the family until I was about eight years of age. Then she got married and moved on. Bobbie was one of the sisters who took care of me at a very young age. We were really close and she was one of my favorite people in the whole world.

Bobbie would bring some of her girl friends home for a visit from time to time. I remember having a crush on many of them. They said I was cute. She later quit school to sing gospel music. But Bobbie decided at a time in the future, to finish high school. And then on to nursing school, she became a registered nurse. A very generous and giving person, Bobbie remains one of my all time favorite people.

Dorothy is next. We called her Dot. She is the sister closest to my age. Consequently, we were sibling rivals. Dot also worked with Da-Cliff and me, in the junk business. In this family, work wasn't assigned on the basis of your sex.

The Family

Dot and I had fights, bicycle races, played ball, and we defied Ma and Da-Cliff. But she was really my partner. As a bicycle rider in the community, she was the best. I will always remember the first time I beat her in a bicycle race.

Dot sought to protect me from the local bullies. And the bullies often whipped both of us in community fights. But we stood together. She was my good friend and closest to me.

Dot was a very good student, but had to quit school because she became pregnant. This changed her life forever. But it also changed mine. In the rural south at that time, communities would ostracize girls who became pregnant. She was forced to quit school and was generally banished from community activities. This left her severely traumatized. And left me not understanding why the community had no heart. I was lost because Dot had no time to be my friend. She had to take care of her child. And I really missed not having her as my buddy. Her living experiences had suddenly become very unhappy. But she always supported me. And I will always support her.

I am next in line and number four from the top. They called me Boot. It is a nickname I have always hated. And this is also the first time I have admitted being called this name. Normally when I am called Boot, I will ignore the caller. I have tried all my life to live down a nickname that I believe have negative connotations. Well in my opinion, it does.

I don't know where this name originated or who the originator was. But I don't like it. And if called by this name, I will not answer.

My family members, and people in the community, had a good time using this name in conjunction with me. So in addition to all my other problems, having a nickname like this didn't help the situation at all.

Brenda is next. She is my sister who did not survive past one year of age. For this reason, I don't know her. But we all remember she was a part of the family.

Jean Audrey is next in line. When she was an adolescent, I was in college. Therefore, we never had the chance to know each other.

Our ideas didn't mesh very well anyway. Maybe there was a bit of a generation gap. Jean, as we called her, was always out of step with me. This certainly contributed to our differing view points. And we still remain generally this way. Well no matter what has happened or what our philosophical differences are, as we age, maybe our view points and ideas will mesh more.

There is another member of the family. She is an unnamed sister who died in childbirth.

Howard is the next oldest boy. We called him Bee. He is a graduate of Clark College in Atlanta, Georgia. Since I am a graduate of Clark College, Bee followed in my footsteps. Well I would like to think that was the case. He has made a really good life for himself in Georgia. I must say he is a very good person and we have grown closer with age.

The youngest person in our family is Winston. He was the best singer and still is in the family. There were many outstanding singers throughout our family, but he had the greatest gift.

There were many ups and downs in Winston's life, but he bounced back from all of them. He has a large family. Well he likes it that way. He is the entrepreneur in our family. And aside from being a good person, he became a Minister.

It was important for me to mention my family. During the turbulent years of my life, the family sustained me. The outside world ridiculed and reviled me. But my family took me in their arms and shielded me from the scorn of others as much as possible. Without this insulation, a much different person from who I am may have emerged.

But aside from my immediate family, the extended one was tremendously important also.

There was a cousin named George Gresham Jr. We called him Clint. Ma's maiden name was Gresham and Clint was the son of her brother. This is significant because Clint grew up as my brother. He came from a broken family, and therefore lived with my family for a while. We hit is off very well right away.

Clint was my constant sidekick. We played football, golf, built huts, rode and fixed bicycles, worked as gardeners, and generally had a good time together. He was the one I related to best, as far as brothers were concerned. I spent more time with him than my natural brothers.

We also had fights together, got beat up together, hustled together, and caddied together.

It is safe to say that we supported each other. Clint was my only real friend, outside of my immediate family unit.

As we grew up, I went to college and he moved to New Jersey. Somehow we grew apart. Maybe the distance had something to do with it. To this day, things have never been the same. And I still don't know why. There was a period of two years in which we never spoke. But I thought of him quite often. It is very sad that we couldn't be brothers throughout our lives or as we got older.

Today, he lives in New Jersey. I use to call him on a regular basis, but I hardly ever saw him. This turned out to be a very painful episode in my life. But our relationship is much better now. This makes me very happy.

There are other cousins who impacted my life. Jim, Ed, and Jeanette Turnipseed are three that come to mind. Their mother was Ma's sister. Their father was Da-Cliff's brother. Since this set of brother married this set of sisters, our families grew up living very close to each other.

Their father named Otis was a really swell person. I had a really good relationship with him. He worked at Delta Airlines with my father. But Da-Cliff had to leave this job because of the chemicals used. Otis stayed with this job and later died from leukemia. I am not sure whether there was a connection or not. But this family was significant in my development. I had fun with Jim, Ed, and Jeanette. We enjoyed many community activities together. Today, we still enjoy a pretty good relationship.

My family, and extended family, lived within a radius of about five miles. We were an extremely large group, numbering in the hundreds.

We visited the members often by just stopping by their homes to say hello, no calling ahead was necessary. Most of the immediate and extended family members lived in the Atlanta area. And I still visit them whenever possible.

In my immediate family, I slept with Bee, my younger brother. This was a fairly normal way of life, especially in the south. There were never enough beds for each individual. Bee would curl up next to me for warmth once we went to bed. No matter how cold it became, my way of sleeping was to stretch out completely. And I didn't want to be touched while I slept. When Bee curled up next to me, I would pinch him.

Now the next morning, he would tell Ma and Da-Cliff. Naturally I would deny it. But Bee would get out of bed crying. And I would say he had a bad dream. Da-Cliff asked me after each complaint, "Did you pinch that boy?" My reply was always an emphatic "No!!" This went on for a long period because they could never catch me in the act. Since I had this angelic and cherubic face, Ma and Da-Cliff couldn't believe that I would pinch anyone.

One evening after going to bed, Bee curled up next to me as usual. I gave him a swift hard pinch. He moved back momentarily, but later curled up next to me again. So I gave him another quick pinch. This went on a few more times. He kept moving closer and I kept pinching. Why is Bee continuing to move closer to me after being pinched so many times? I began to question myself about this. Well a light were beginning to click on in my thick skull.

So I reached over and touched his arm. Boy, it seemed awfully large. So I touched it a few more times and was shocked to learn, this was Da-Cliff. I had been pinching my father all night. Now he had busted me. I was caught in the act and I didn't sleep for the rest of the night, because of what was going to happen in the morning.

Da-Cliff awakened early the next morning. But I slept later than usual. He waited patiently until I decided to get out of bed. He allowed me to eat breakfast. But all during breakfast, he had this smirk on his face and I knew exactly what was going on. This was mental and emotional torture and Da-Cliff was letting me stew in it.

Well it finally happened. Da-Cliff scolded me for the long period of torture heaped upon Bee. And I felt really bad about it. Now I was sent out to retrieve a small branch from a tree, called a switch. With this switch, Da-Cliff gave me the whipping of my life.

From that day to now, I have never pinched anyone. I was cured. Now as I reminisce about this, it is kind of funny. But I am sorry for the pain my brother had to endure.

We moved many times in Clayton County. Most of the early homes were shanty types. And once we moved near a swamp. This was scary because we had to deal with Snakes everyday. We drank water from a natural spring. And it was very good. But in route to the spring, Dot and I would always encounter several snakes. We were scared to death, but this became our way of life.

When chores were assigned to us, they had to be done. Those were the rules growing up in the rural south. So we learned to deal with those situations. We banged tin cans and made as much noise as possible to scare the snakes away. They moved and our route was cleared.

In addition to the snakes, there were bats. Sometimes the bats would invade our house and we quickly vacated it. Da-Cliff would take a broom and shoo the bats out. This method was very effective. During the time living in this house, there was one adventure after another. In retrospect, it was fun.

There were no streetlights, no paved roads, no running water and no indoor plumbing. At night, it was really dark. So Dot and I never went out of the house at night. We were scared to do so.

A syrup mill was also nearby. So one day, Dot took me to the syrup mill to play. Her friend Harvey joined us. Now at the syrup mill, sugar cane was pushed through a sausage type grinder. The juice coming from the cane was used to make syrup. The pulley used to grind the cane was usually hooked up to a horse. And the horse would pull the whole assembly in a circular motion.

This could be dangerous, so you had to keep alert. I was very young at that time. So Dot and Harvey decided to grind a few sticks of cane. Dot decided to pull the assembly while Harvey pushed the cane through the grinder. So the process proceeded. All of a sudden I heard screaming, "Stop, stop, help, help!!!"

Neither Dot nor I knew what was happening. Harvey had pushed the cane too far into the grinder. Dot not knowing this, kept the pulley moving. But those screams sounded so scary.

Dot had cut off Harvey's fingers. So I moved closer to Harvey to investigate. There was blood everywhere. Suddenly, there were these four fingers lying on the ground under the grinder. I yelled, "Dot stop!" She stopped the pulley and ran over to us. When she saw what had happened, a look appeared on her face that I hadn't seen before. Dot staggered as if to faint, then suddenly recovered somewhat. Harvey was uncontrollably screaming and Dot probably realized that someone had to get help. I was really too small to run for help. So Dot told me to stay with Harvey and she ran down the road yelling, "Help, help, help."

While Dot was gone, I was really frightened. Looking at Harvey's face, I didn't know whether he was going to live or die, and not knowing what to do, I could only watch him wince in pain.

Suddenly after what seemed like an eternity, Dot returned with Da-Cliff and a few neighbors. She came over to me, took my hand and led me away from the commotion. I could see that she was also severely traumatized, but was trying to be brave. Although being very young, I could since a change come over Dot that day. The pain of this incident lingered with her for many years.

Meanwhile, Da-Cliff and the neighbors were taking care of Harvey. They wrapped his hand and rushed him to the hospital. But they left his fingers on the ground. Dot and I stared at each other and at the fingers in disbelief. A neighbors saw us standing there looking scared and confused, so he took us home.

After things settled down, Dot received a severe whipping. I felt sorry for her because she didn't mean for this to happen. It was an accident that was nobody's fault. After Dot's whipping, I tried to console her with a hug. But I was too small, so I hugged her legs. I believe this incident bonded us closer together.

The Family

At a point in the future, Harvey recovered physically from this accident. I don't know what happened mentally. I couldn't imagine the type of adjustment he would have to make for the rest of his life, as a result of this accident.

But soon after Harvey's recovery, he and his family moved away. They didn't want to live near my family anymore. Although they didn't blame my sister for this accident, they decided to move anyway. Well in those times, families moved their residences quite often.

A few months later, my family decided to move. Well I can say moving away from this snake infested swamp, with all its bad memories, made me very happy.

We moved closer to my grandfather. My cousins, Jim, Ed, and Jeanette also lived across the street from us at the new location. They had large pecan and pear trees in their yard. Their house was a shanty type, and is still standing.

I have always loved pecans and pears. Willie Lou, the mother of my cousins, would not share any nuts or fruit with my family.

I could never understand this at all, because they had more than enough. And she knew that I loved pecans. So I would sneak over and steal some anyway.

With all the moving my family did, we were never lucky enough to have a pecan or a pear tree in our yard. I played with my cousins many times, but was forbidden to take any pears or pecans.

Living close to my grandfather afforded me the opportunity to spend more time on his farm. His name was Beasley Gresham. He was an extremely handsome man with a bald head and deep brown eyes. His reputation was that of a really brutal person. But I never saw that side of him. Well maybe being so young, helped cloud my image of him. I didn't witness much brutality at all. Ma told me about a whipping he gave me when I was eight months old. I was crawling and knocked over the slop bucket used for feeding hogs. I asked Ma, "How can you whip a baby?" Her answer," this was his way." I didn't know about this until Ma told me. So I wanted to go to his grave, dig him up, and punch him in the nose. It was normal for children to get whippings at that time, but not babies. But Ma told me if you went against his will, he would hit you with the first thing he put his hands on. Then he would keep hitting you until he felt like quitting or became tired. Well he was generally kind to me. And maybe he didn't want to show his brutal side and kept it from me. But his farm was the nerve center for the entire family. And grandfather, Big Pop as we called him, was the patriarch of our entire clan. Therefore time spent at Big Pop's place, was quite enjoyable. I remember him and the family moving twice. Both farmhouses were Victorian type. One of these farmhouses, that I liked very much, had a huge Magnolia tree out back.

This farm is where I would spend a great deal of time. Catching Tadpoles and Salamanders in a nearby brook, was a daily ritual while visiting grandfather at this house. There were brooks and streams everywhere.

But snakes and rats were around also. One of these snakes bit my older sister Bobbie on the toe. But I it wasn't poisonous. While on the farm, I was chased by goats, dogs, bats, pigs, and bulls. I fell out of trees, was thrown by mules and horses, and was strung by wasps and bees many times. To me, this was normal. It happened on all farms.

Being poor, we didn't wear shoes during the summer, unless going to church. We cut our feet and stubbed our toes many times. Kerosene was the great chemical that cured everything. And in my young life, many more things happened to me.

Once down on my grandfather's farm, I was literally hanged. I went into the corral where horses, cows, and mules were kept. The gate was open. As I attempted to go through behind my step grandmother, it began to close. Now it was a really heavy gate and there was a huge hook it. The hook was just swinging in the breeze. As I went through, this hook snared me in the neck under my chin. Since I was not very heavy, it lifted me right off the ground. I suddenly found myself swinging in the breeze. The world seemed to be floating all around me. What a weird feeling. During all this commotion, I never lost consciousness. But I was frightened very much because I didn't know what to do. Actually, I couldn't do anything.

The Family

Suddenly, there were scream coming from everywhere. Ma came running. Big Pop and other aunts and uncles arrived about the same time. All were screaming and yelling. "Get that boy down from there." I was still swinging like a rag doll.

Now I felt all these hands grasping at me. Some seemed to be pulling while other was pushing. But I was lifted to relieve the pressure on my neck. Now the hook was removed. Then a cloth was placed over the wound. But now there was immense pain. And I could just barely stand it. But Ma and the rest of my family tried to make me as comfortable as possible. I was rushed to the hospital to be patched up.

Well surgery was required to close my wound. As I awakened after the surgical procedure, Ma's face was the first one I saw. And it was a pleasant sight. "How do you feel boy," she asked? At that moment, Ma looked at me with such love in her eyes. This look made me feel kind of funny but very warm. I have never forgotten this moment and never will.

Well I was one lucky little boy. The doctors said if the hook had snared me one inch farther back in the neck, my esophagus would have been torn out. The hook had embedded into the fleshy area in the front of my neck under my chin. Well besides being one frightened little boy, I lived to tell about this experience.

My family moved again. Since we had moved several times before, it didn't bother me at all. Each time we had moved, it seemed to be for the better. But there was an enormous pasture in the front of this house. We could walk through the pasture, to our home, or walk one mile around it. Dot and I always walked through. There were goats and bulls lurking nearby.

And we were chased many times by these animals. After being chased a few times by this particular goat, I decided to do something about it. Goats would normally eat anything. So this day I fed him a few hot peppers. At this point, he went wild, running, jumping, kicking and all sorts of things.

This was quite funny to me. In fact, Dot and I both had a good laugh about it. I was probably going to do it again, but Dot told Ma about it. Well I received a good whipping for my efforts.

While living in this house, Dot and I got into one dilemma after another. We took the wagon for a joyride one day. Since we were not authorized to use it, of course something happened. We turned it over. To my amazement, we did not get a whipping. I guess Ma and Da-cliff were happy to see us alive. Well we didn't stay in that house very long. And I was happy to move. Too many goats and bulls were around.

ADOLESCENCE AND HIGH SCHOOL

We moved into my favorite house. It was white and really pretty small. In all our moving, the family never had a house large enough for everybody. But it was still a very pleasant home.

I had many unusual experiences while living in this house on White Line Street. There was a haunted church next door. We played on the church property by day, but wouldn't go near it at night. The church yard also became our ball field. I had much fun there because it was a gathering place visited at some point, by most of the kids in the neighborhood.

Well one day while working on the foundation of our new house, Da-Cliff disturbed a nest of rats. They scattered all over the place. And a few nights later, one of the disoriented rats got loose in the house. Somehow while I was sleeping, the rat crawled into my bed and bit me in the head. I screamed, "Ooooh, ooooh, oooohu."

Responding to my screams, all the family members jumped out of bed. Da-Cliff not knowing what had happened, rushed into my room with his shotgun. I yelled, "A rat bit me in the head." Well I was more frightened than hurt. There was a bit of blood. So Ma took a towel, dabbed it in kerosene, and put it on my head. She said to kill the germs. We were all shaken up by this incident. And something had to be done. So the covers were stripped from the beds, and no rat was found. All corners of the house were searched for the stray rat. Again, he was not found. Now when the commotion was all over, there was no more sleeping that night, in this house.

A really concerned Ma and Da-Cliff, took me to the doctor in the morning. I was given an injection and pills to take for the next few days. And no long-range effects from this incident occurred. But I did maintain a fear of rodents. Da-Cliff would eventually find and destroy the nest of rats living under our house. And this problem never arose again.

By now, I was starting high school. The new house was nearer to where I took the bus. There was a white high school about one half mile from where I lived. But of course we could not attend. Blacks had to walk to a predetermined location. From there we were bussed to the colored high school, about twenty miles away.

High school would prove to be one of the most agonizing periods in my life. I went to William Alfred Fountain High School. It was a completely new school and many kids in the surrounding communities were students there.

Although it was a new school, supplies were not in great abundance. Meager resources were more like it. We had hand-me-down books from the local white high school. This happened throughout my entire high school career. The white high school would get a supply of new books.

The colored high school, would receive the old books from the white school. If the white high school didn't receive any new book, the colored high school didn't receive any books at all.

But when it did happen, a truck from the white high school would deliver a load of books to the library in the colored school. This was literally a mess. Teachers from various departments within the school would converge on the library in search of books for their classes. Talking about confusion, this was it. This was how teachers supplied their classes because no new supplies were forthcoming. The colored high school didn't receive any new supplies.

I remember playing football in a hand-me-down uniform. Coaches from the white high school loaded a truck with their old uniforms. These uniforms were delivered to our school and dumped on the gymnasium floor. Our football team would pillage through this pile of mostly rubbish to try and find a uniform that could be used.

These uniforms were then held together by lots of tape. Shoulder and hip pads were repaired with wire. Can you imagine this happening? In the south at that time, it happened on too many occasions.

After the delivery of these old uniforms, the white superintendent of schools would appear. He would smile in our faces, shake our principal's hand, and congratulate him on receiving these old supplies. The superintendent acted as if he was doing us a favor, yet knowing how he was belittling us. Typing paper was the only new supplies received by our school. I thought this situation was pretty pathetic. I also had a pretty low opinion of the schools superintendent.

The school was very poor, but it was the only one we had. So I got use to this and just settled into a regular routine. This reinforced what I already knew. There was no emphasis placed on educating colored students. This reality would be reinforced from time to time, during my entire high school career. This was racism, but facing negative racial behavior was commonplace.

All during this time, I was a pronounced stutterer. This embarrassed me a lot. It changed my life greatly, because the students talked about me much of the time. I was generally afraid to participate in any social activities.

Going to school was fun, but it was also very stressful. I would sit in the back of the classroom, trying to hide from the teacher. If I didn't understand something about the subject matter, I was afraid to raise my hand to ask for a further explanation. In school, teachers expected class participation from students. But I always had a difficult time expressing myself. Ar-ar-ar, ar, and th-th-th- were the ways most of my sentences began. Consequently, a lot of things I wanted to say just went unsaid. This was very frustrating and unfulfilling. And throughout my high school career, situations like this, was part of what I had to deal with.

Alfred Douglas Turnipseed

I joined the basketball team, well sort of. Most of the team members were very tall. I was five feet three inches tall. And I weighed about one hundred and fifteen pounds. Plus, I had no talent. But at that time, I believed just the contrary. I didn't get into games even during practice. But I kept trying thinking my chance to play would come.

We played a very bad team one night. All during the game, my team was way ahead in score. All the other players had gotten a chance to play in the game. Then with about fifteen seconds left in the game, the coach said, "Turnipseed get in there." I couldn't believe my ears. What embarrassment! Meekly, I entered the game amidst much laughter. The game ended just about the time I walked onto the floor. All I wanted to do was run and hide. I took much longer to get dressed, because I wanted most of the fans, my peers, and other team members to have left the gymnasium when I emerged. Getting dressed early meant I would hear all the taunts, teases, and the ridicule. But I was trying to fit in.

The basketball team consisted of twelve varsity players. The road uniforms were dark and the home uniforms were white. When the team went on the road, I did not dress for the games. Well I didn't go to the games at all. But when the team played home games, I dressed in a road uniform. This meant I was not going to play. It was also quite embarrassing. Clearly I had to make a change, and find another way to fit in.

The solution came to me one night in a dream. I quit the team as a player and became the trainer. This position is simply a gofer for the coach. Helping the players with their uniforms, supplying them with water, were duties associated with this job. I didn't mind this and it was fun going to all games both home and away.

During my first year in high school, I touched a girl for the first time. All classrooms had a Cloakroom for storing coats, hats, wraps, and boots. About three o'clock, students went to the cloakroom to retrieve their coats and hats.

This day, a girl named Shirley happened to be in the cloakroom. Many boys were in the cloakroom also. She let all the boys, who wanted to, feel and touch her. I was overjoyed. For the first time in life, I had an erection. A hard on is what we called it. What a strange feeling! I felt her breasts and in between her legs. She seemed to be enjoying it, and many boys were participating. I watched the other boys to find out what to do next. But they squeezed me out, so I left her there with them. I don't know what they did to her or with her. This opportunity never presented itself again. Shirley thought I was the dumbest boy she has ever encountered. And now I think she was right. I tried to avoid her because of the constant teasing. Whenever the opportunity arose, she took great pleasure pulling up her dress, to expose a pair of great looking legs and everything else to me. But I could never touch her again. She really tortured me.

Also during my first year in high school, many other things happened. A boy in my class, Willie Mason, started a feud with me. It would last throughout my high school career. He teased me about stuttering, my hair, my clothes, and my lack of knowledge concerning girls. We fought constantly. Later, his sister and brother joined in the harassment of me. They made my high school days very difficult, to say the least. But I kept going.

There were always school functions. The standard dress for boys was a dark suit. Ma had a credit account with the Gay Clothing Company.

So she purchased me a blue suit. I was very proud of it. Going to church, to school plays, concerts, and to dances, a dark suit was always in style. Ma made a great sacrifice to purchase this suit. It probably cost about ten or twelve dollars. And that was a lot of money for a family of our means. I always cherished that suit.

Another great tragic event happened during this time. One morning I left for school along with my brothers and sisters. The family went through its regular routines. Ma and Da-Cliff went to work. Nothing unusual happened to me during the day. So I left for home after school.

My family lived on the corner of White Line Street just around a sharp curve. Rounding this curve looking toward my home as usual, I saw nothing. My home had disappeared. I was looking at space. It took me a few moments to realize what had happened. The house had burned down. And the only thing left standing was a chimney.

My knees buckled. My heart fluttered, and tears began streaming down my face. I felt as if someone had stabbed me in the heart. I was trembling all over. A few people in the community rushed over in an effort to help me. Ma and Da-Cliff hadn't yet arrived home. Therefore, I was all alone in my grief and hysteria. And I was hysterical. Neighbors were still trying to console me, but to no avail. I had no place to go, and no place to hide. Everything was all gone.

I sat on the side of the street in a daze. This wasn't happening. Somehow, it had to be a bad dream. I closed my eyes and squeezed them tightly together trying to block out this bad dream.

But when I opened them, the bad dream persisted. This was real and the pain of it was real. I continued to sit alone on the curb and cry. How much more could I endure? Would these painful episodes continue to happen in my life? I have had so many, my mind thought. Again, I felt like a little boy alone in the world.

My sister Dot arrived a short time later. She went through the same agony, I had just experienced. We just cried and held on to each other because the pain was almost unbearable. My toys, clothes, family pictures, keepsakes, were all gone. But more importantly, I had no home. The little white house that I loved so much, with a saw mill in the back yard, where I was bitten by a rat, next to the haunted church, would never be my safe haven again. I was a very sad little boy.

Dot and I didn't know what to do or expect. People around us were crying and were befuddled as to what should be done. This led to more confusion for Dot and I. We prayed for Ma and Da-Cliff to hurry and get home to comfort and keep us safe again.

But can you imagine how it felt to have left your home on a particular site, and now peering into open space? This is a sight I will never forget for as long as I live. The bicycle Ma had struggled to purchase for me, my air rifle with the telescope, also had been lost.

In the midst of my misery, Ma and Da-cliff finally arrived. All the emotions generated earlier were replayed. Ma screamed and tried to shield us I suppose, from her pain. Da-Cliff tried to console us all. Now the whole family was crying and holding on to each other. We believed at this point, there was nothing else left to hold on to.

Ma never recovered from the loss of our home. But as she stood crying, I wanted to comfort her. So looking up into her face I said, "don't cry Ma, I will buy you another house. So please don't worry." In the midst of her grief, Ma gave me the most loving look and the best hug ever. She knew her little boy really meant it. And it did seem to offer her a bit of comfort. Da-Cliff didn't express too much emotion about our lost home, except for when he first saw it. I believe he felt powerless to do anything or the pain was just too great. He never spoke of our lost home again.

After the confusion was over, we were thankful to have each other and to be alive. No one was hurt, but we lost all of our worldly possessions.

A few days later, we realized something had been saved. My blue suit was in the dry cleaners. We rejoiced and considered this a good sign. Maybe this suit had special magical powers. It became a rallying symbol for the family. We had many family crises after losing our home. When this happened, we would touch the suit. Somehow through its magical powers, things seemed to get better. Because of this, I never wore the suit again.

The next few days and weeks were upsetting and filled with uncertainty. My stable environment had been upset. So we had to live with relatives. Dot and I lived with our cousins, M. T. and Catherine Starr. My other brothers and sisters lived with Otis and Willie Lou Turnipseed, our uncle and aunt.

Ma and Da-Cliff lived with Big Pop, our grandfather. These relatives made my family as comfortable as possible. But we felt out of place.

My family was at the mercy of the community. But I must say the whole community, black and white, responded to our basic needs. There were seven members of my family living together when this tragedy occurred. This made it impossible for us to live together in one relative's household. Being split up, made things more difficult for Ma and Da-Cliff, because they had to check on all the children before going to work.

But I must say, we had more clothing and toys than prior to our tragedy. Everything we had was new, but it just didn't feel right. Imagine playing in new clothes. I longed for the old stuff.

Living with different relatives made it difficult for my family to stay in touch, but we tried. Loneliness was becoming a factor for me and the rest of the family.

Ma and Da-Cliff busied themselves during the next few weeks, securing suitable housing for the family. They found a place in the same community, and this would be our home until I graduated from college. The community and the Red Cross supported my family by donating furniture for our new house. We had better furniture than before. But the old stuff was still more comfortable.

We were finally back together again. This was one of the happiest days of my life. I will never forget how the neighbors supported us during this most difficult period. Even today, my family has very close ties to this community.

I liked the new home for one very good reason. It sat on a large tract of land. But this house was not as good or as beautiful as the previous one. But Ma said we should feel blessed to have this one, and to be together again. Ma had a way of making us feel better in most situations. But I loved the huge tract of land and really enjoyed it.

I built a three-hole golf course on this property. And my eight-foot high basketball goal was set up there. This is really where I grew up. And in the next few months, life took on some semblance of normalcy. My really big regret, even now, is never being able to buy Ma a new house. We have had many conversations about this. Now it was really never an issue with Ma, but she helped to resolve it in my mind. I have deemed it a failure on my part. And I am still very sorry about it.

Ma purchased me a new suit from Gay Clothiers. It was an English Tweed, and was quite different from my previous suit. But I grew to love it because Ma sacrificed for me to have it. Life was more stable now. But I still had to work to help support myself. New shoes were needed to accentuate my new suit.

So I took a job working with my cousin Clint, as a gardener. We were both in high school and could certainly manage working in flower gardens. We worked for two very old sisters, who were white, in Jonesboro Georgia. They had a huge Victorian house that seemed to date back to the revolutionary period. These sisters were about eighty years old. To boys thirteen and sixteen, they were ancient.

Both had really long gray hair, long faces, were very skinny, and looked like witches, at least in our thirteen and sixteen year old minds.

One of the sisters sent Clint and I up to the attic one day to remove some rubbish. Ascending the stairs and reaching the attic, we looked around this spooky room. And it seemed as if time has stood still in there. Among the relics were pictures of old men and women. There were old books under layers of dust. There was old furniture and many old clothes. Now the pictures of the old men and women seemed to be staring directly at us and following our every move. This was really creepy.

Suddenly we heard a noise. Turning in the direction of the noise, we saw a really old woman with long gray hair hanging straight down over her face. We thought she was a witch. My cousin and I were scared out of our wits. We both started to scream. The witch came closer and closer to us. And we were really frightened. I felt as if my curly hair was standing straight up. She came directly up to us and we realized this was one of the sisters we worked for. What a relief. Wow, now this was one scary experience Clint and I never forgot. "What was all the screaming about?" She inquired. We saw a huge rat, was our reply. I don't know whether she accepted this explanation or not, but we were certainly shaken up by this whole episode. We continued to work for these sisters for the next few years.

Clint and I also worked as caddies at the local golf course. One day at the course, I was urged to wrestle with a white boy.

Now in the Deep South during this period, white women, girls, and boys, weren't bothered, especially if there were white men around. But the white men were the ones urging me to wrestle this boy. I guess they thought he was going to beat me up. So I kept refusing and they pushed him onto me.

The white boy grabbed me and started tussling. Since I wasn't going to let him take advantage of me, I tussled back. Now we started to wrestle. I picked him up and threw him down. Although being small, I was very strong. With the full force of my weight, I came down on the boy breaking his collarbone. He screamed very loudly. Hearing the commotion, other men rushed in to see what was happening. Now I thought the white men would attack me, but they didn't. The boy was taken to the hospital. And the white men never urged anyone else to wrestle me again. I continued to be their caddy and there were no repercussions from this incident. But Clint was pretty scared.

The first year of high school passed with no other major event occurring. My stuttering was just as bad. I had no girlfriend. I was a virgin. The outside world didn't affect me at all. My family was still very poor. There was no place for me in this world. Other than those things, my life was normal.

My second year in high began with a bang. I was involved in a fight with Willie Mason. We fought over his knack of teasing me about stuttering. He ripped my shirt and I bit him on the forehead. We both spent the next day in the principle's office. And Ma whipped me for fighting in school. Yes, my parents whipped me until I graduated from high school.

I joined the student government association. But I don't remember what my job or duties were. It was probably a non-speaking job.

My speaking skills on a scale of one to ten, was about a two. But somehow, I just wanted to be involved.

The high school chorus was my next venture. Since I always loved music, I auditioned for it and passed. Now my chorus future was set. But the director wasn't very good. We sang elementary songs and student interest was at an all time low.

In the middle of the year, the chorus director was fired. Then a new director from New Jersey was hired. His name was Mr. Sewett. From the very first day, the changes were immediately felt. My whole outlook on music changed.

I didn't know what classical music was. In fact, I hadn't heard of classical music. Bach, Beethoven, and the other masters were names I hadn't ever heard. Until my second year in high school, I hadn't ever heard a symphony orchestra play, or ever heard of an opera. Mr. Sewett changed all of that. He introduced us to a new form of music. This had a profound affect upon me. We sang music composed by the great masters. And we listened to symphonic music and were introduced to opera.

This was the beginning of my music education that has continued to this day. The chorus entered and won many competitions. It became a source of pride for the whole community. Now the school was relatively small, but the chorus developed a statewide reputation for excellence.

During the next two years, my chorus experiences reached new heights. Accolades poured in from many sources around the state.

And there were invitations to compete in national choral competitions. Musically things were great, until Mr. Sewett died in the middle of my senior year. He died from cirrhosis of the liver, literately drinking himself to death. We were hurt and surprised by this turn of events. Now I was beginning to learn other people had problems to. But I was happy Mr. Sewett had come into my life, because he opened a door to the wonderful world of music. For this, I will always remember him fondly.

After his death the chorus was never the same, while I was a student at Fountain High School. But my thirst for music had been fueled. It gave me a feeling of being connected to something greater than myself. A sense of beauty, and music was beautiful in my eyes. So I joined the school's band. Ma purchased a new French horn for me because the band director suggested it. And my career as a French horn player was born. I would play this instrument for many years to come.

Now our high school band wasn't very good. We didn't have enough instruments for the interested students. And we were all beginners. In the elementary schools where we came from, there were no music programs. But we did our best.

The cost of my French horn was two hundred and twenty-five dollars. This was an exorbitant amount of money during this period. Since my family was extremely poor, this was quite an investment on Ma's part. She had very good credit, often paying one dollar a week on her account. I know Ma made a great sacrifice to purchase this instrument. And I was very grateful. But to this day, it boggles my mind as to how she accomplished this while earning only fifteen dollars a week as a domestic. But Ma sacrificed for all of us. In her words, she wanted us to have a better chance than she had. Somehow Ma could make impossible things work.

My singing debut as a soloist was made during the second year of high school. I used to sit back in my room listening to country and western music. Back in my high school days, it was called Hillbilly music. Ma questioned me often as to why I listened to this type of music. But I loved it. So my debut was made singing a hillbilly song. The name was. "I Don't Know Why I Should Cry Over You?" by Gene Autry. Well it turned out fairly well.

So later in other singing engagements, I sang hillbilly songs. One of my favorites was, "Wondering Who's Kissing You," by Hank Williams". So my reputation in school became that of a hillbilly singer.

But later I turned to singing the blues. But Hillbilly music was my favorite. These songs are still fresh in my memory and I can still sing them. Since one doesn't stutter while singing, I had found a way for self expression.

Three other boys and I formed a singing group. Mark and Ward Reade, Fred (Nat) Robinson, and I were a Doo Wop group known as The Warriors. We patterned ourselves after other famous groups, like The Midnighters, The Moon Glows, and The Flamingos. We were extremely good and sang in many local night clubs in and around Atlanta. Our reputation was really growing.

Friday and Saturday nights we performed in nightclubs. On Sundays, we performed in local churches around Atlanta singing gospel music. Ma told me this was a sin. But I didn't think so. I just loved music and it didn't matter to me what type.

Retrospectively, I would've liked a career in music, especially singing, but it was not my focus at that point. In our singing group, each of us had a different agenda. Mark was the oldest. He was a senior, very much in love, and wanted to get married right away.

Many singing arrangements, for the group, were pinned by Mark. For the most part, he was our lead singer. Ward, Mark's bother was the tenor. He had the most talent of anyone in the group. His voice was similar to that of Johnny Mathis. This boy could really sing. Talent scouts from the Ted Mack Amateur Hour liked him very much. So they scheduled Ward to appear on the amateur show in New York City.

For reasons unknown to the rest of the group, Ward didn't take advantage of this great opportunity. I sang baritone in the group. Now I was not the leader Mark was, not blessed with the great voice like Ward, and not as versatile as Fred, I just offered a steady rich tone needed to cement the other voices together. Fred sang bass most of the time. But he occasionally sang the lead part. He had the least amount of talent in the group, but was the most comical.

Mark wanted to get married. Ward had no future plans. Fred would get into drugs. I would continue my schooling. We were all very different. But at this point in our lives, all the parts worked very well. And we performed throughout my high school career and had a great reputation around the city of Atlanta. Had we stuck with it, this could've been one of the really great Doo Wop groups of the world. But we had fun while it lasted.

Girls followed the group regularly and we loved it. Whenever we performed, our favorite expression was, "make the girl pee on themselves." We actually just wanted the girls to like us. Maybe it doesn't make any sense today, but it motivated us then.

Also during my second year in high school, Big Pop moved to another farm. The Magical Magnolia Tree, that had been my safe haven for years, was gone. I was depressed and left with a sense of depravation and loss. Could I find a place with the same calming affect, a place where I felt safe, a place where I could express myself, a place of reverence? Well I never found another such a place.

I visited Big Pop regularly, and really loved his new farm. It had a large porch that wrapped around the entire house. And there were many fruit trees, but no pecan trees. On the weekends and during school breaks, I would spend as much time as possible on his farm.

The houses of both farms are still standing. I often drive by both and reminisce, when in the Atlanta area. Around those farms where fields lay stretched in the distance, when I was growing up, are now housing developments. Well they call this progress. But I can still hear sounds from my childhood and other family events, when I drive by those houses.

But many other events were happening during my second year of high school. I joined the football team. There was no good equipment for me, or any other player. We used hand-me down football uniforms and other equipment. My weight was up to about one hundred and twenty pounds. So the coach didn't take me very seriously. He figured, one hard tackle from one of the really huge player, I would quit.

One day he had me line up against this huge player named Bobby Mays. He must've weighed about two hundred fifty pounds at least. He was to tackle me while I was standing still. So I braced for the impact, and it came. As he hit me, every bone in my body rattled. His full weigh came crashing down on me like a Mack truck, burying me in the earth. All eyes were on me, and the coach watched in anticipation of my departure. I picked myself up and yelled these words to this huge player. "Can't you hit any harder than that?" and, "would you like to try it again?"

The team and the coach were amazed. I was waved to the sideline. But I was very happy the huge player didn't take me up on the offer of another hit. He left me quaking in my shoes and in much pain. But none of the other players knew this. Had he said yes to my offer,

I might have quit. Needless to say, I made the team. And the coach never questioned my courage again. I was a starter in my first year of playing organized football.

My very first game was a disaster. We played a team in Griffin Georgia, and they had a lighted stadium. My team had never played under those conditions. We had only played in an open field. They kicked off to us to start the game. I received the kick from the opposing team.

As they kicked the ball, I looked up into the lights and lost sight of everything. The ball hit me in the chest and bounced back up field toward the opponents. They promptly recovered the ball and scored a few plays later. The coach looked toward me and tried to calm the team.

They kicked off again, and the ball headed in my direction. As I tried to catch it, something happened.

The ball ricocheted off my chest back in the direction of the opponents. Again, the opposing team recovered the ball and scored a few plays later. By now, the coach was seething.

He sat me on the bench and I stayed there for the entire season. He had lost faith in my ability and this affected me greatly. But I still believed in my ability. What I lacked was experience. Somehow the team managed to finish the season. We lost all our games. After the season was over, the school year seemed to move very slowly. So I decided to make studies my number one priority.

Mazel Owend was my sophomore homeroom teacher. She was very kind and encouraging. Although the school was not staffed in terms of college counselors, most teachers encouraged us to prepare for college. This was indicative of most colored schools, in the Deep South at that time.

On one of my visits to New York, my cousins who lived there and I discussed this encouragement issue at length. Their experience in high school, in New York City was this. Counselors encouraged and steered black students into commercial and automotive courses. So I was thankful for our kind of teachers. In our segregated schools, in the

Deep South, since all school personal was black, students were steered toward academics courses. Even in New York during this period, educating black students was not a priority of the controlling white administrators. And in my opinion, it is still the same.

Colored schools had meager resources, but black teachers urged their students to look ahead, go to college, and to use these resources to the best of their abilities. I was very fond of Ms. Owend and other teachers of this era.

They tried to instill us with pride by constantly introducing us to great Black American who had an impact on society. They wanted all the students to know, there were black heroes. Now for this enlightenment, I will never forget them.

Later that year, I joined the Boy Scouts. Aside from my studies, football, the band, the chorus and the Doo Wop group, scouting became very important to me. It gave me a chance to learn some practical skills like, swimming, leadership, survivorship and many others. Being involved in those many activities, gave my life some meaning.

Camping was one of my favorite activities. For seven dollars and fifty cent, I could spend a week at a Boy Scout camp. This was really fun. It gave me a chance to meet boys my own age, from all over the state of Georgia. A week away from home and from the ridicule of my friends was just what I needed. Scouting over the next few years, became very important to me in my quest to become a productive human being.

I developed a feud with this boy named Henry Rogers. He was a handsome young boy about two grades ahead of me in school. He was also a boy scout. But I could sense that major trouble was on the horizon with him.

One evening during a scout meeting, we had an argument. Now all scout meetings were held on school property. Our meeting was in a room with a foundation about eight feet off the ground. So we had to walk up about eight stairs to the meeting room. Now Henry began to tease me about my stuttering and this started the argument.

I said hello to one of the other boy scouts. Since I stuttered, the first word was "Ha-ha-ha-ha-hey." Hey is the way we said hello. At this point, Henry butted in and said. "Keep quite you no talking Bastard?" I tried to answer him, but stuttering defeated me once again. He called me a few more ugly names. Then he told me I had big eyes, had hair like BB shots, because of the separation of my hair, and that I was a tar baby (black), because of the color of my skin. In those days, black was not considered beautiful. Henry was a light skinned black boy. These statements elicited laughter from some of the other scouts. Since the meeting was about to start, the whole episode was over, so I thought. Now when the meeting was over, I turned to go down the flight of stairs.

Suddenly I was airborne. He had kicked me down the stairs. And at this point, I didn't know what had happened. As I hit the ground, he jumped right on me. Landing on the ground from such a surprised attack had caused me to become disoriented. He immediately began to hit me. His first blow landed on my temple. This punch had muddled the clarity of my mind. So my ability to think had been compromised. He literally rained blows all over my head and body. Suddenly realizing I couldn't do anything, panic overtook me. My life would be in jeopardy if this assault continued much longer. So I prayed to God that he would find some way to keep this boy from killing me.

In the meantime, blows were coming from everywhere. I couldn't see them at all, but I felt every one of them. The constant pounding against my head was taking its toll. So I prayed again. "God, please help me! Please, please help me!" I staggered while trying to get on my feet. Well Henry continued to hit me. As I tried once again to stand up, Henry kicked me in the chest.

The force of this blow sent me reeling onto a sharp object. I don't know what this object was, but I felt it pierce my right arm. The pain was almost unbearable, and when I looked at my arm, it was split wide open. Then one of the others scouts shouted "he's bleeding." Then suddenly, Henry stopped beating me. God had heard my cry and my supplication. I was actually happy this sharp object had slit my arm. Otherwise, he might have been beating me forever, or until he had killed me.

I was thinking. Where was the Scout Master? Why hadn't he stopped this massacre? Well maybe he had left the meeting before the attack had started. But this has always been a mystery to me.

After recovering somewhat, I was able to go to the bathroom. Blood was all over my arm and hand. What was I to do at this point? Being a boy scout, I had to think, get control of my wits.

So I removed my underwear, tore them into strips, and wrapped them tightly around my wound. This stopped the bleeding. And I washed the excess blood from my arm and hand and then went home. Well sneaked home was more like it. I didn't want any family member to know about this incident.

After arriving home, I cleaned my wound with kerosene. Remember kerosene is the chemical used for every hurt, pain, or scratch. So after cleaning, I carefully wrapped my arm with a cloth.

I wore long sleeved shirts for the next three to four months until my arm healed. This was during the spring and summer months, so it was quite a hassle. The questions were many. And most people thought I was crazy to wear long sleeved shirt in the hot weather.

But I was successful at keeping this incident a secret. The other boys also kept quiet about it. Maybe they felt guilty for not coming to my rescue.

But Ma never knew about this incident until years and years later. Today I have this ugly scar on my right arm. Now since this wound was never repaired, it never healed properly. I certainly wasn't going to a doctor to get sewn up. Then the whole community would've known, including Ma.

On my visits to Atlanta, I often see Henry Rogers. He is about one hundred and twenty pounds and is also an alcoholic. Well that word is too nice for him. A drunk is more like it. Whenever I lay eyes on him, the urge to beat him up is a tremendous temptation. Because the beating he administered to me, as a kid, is still vivid in my mind. But he is in enough pain, and no pleasure would be derived from beating up a drunk.

Thinking back about this incident, when my arm had healed, a few of the local boys asked me this question. "Are you going to get him back, seek revenge?" My reply was, "Are you crazy?" If I go back to seek revenge, and this boy beats me up again, he might kill me. So at that time, I didn't take any further action. But it has certainly crossed my mind many times.

The dispute should've ever taken place. But I now know why his dislike for me was so strong. He wanted to sing my part in the Doo Wop group. And two members of the group, Mark and Ward, were his cousins. But I could sing the part better. Therefore, it was mine. Never getting a chance to sing this part, he took a very negative attitude toward me. I guess he just took those frustrations out, by beating me up.

Later that same year, I beat up a boy. But he deserved it. This older boy had assaulted Jean, my youngest sister. He tried to kiss and fondle her, but she resisted and ran home.

Finding out about this, I immediately began to search for this boy. Upon finding him, I launched a swift attack, really beating him up. Man, I was just crazy with anger. While pounding him, he didn't lift a finger in defense. So after becoming tired from such a vigorous attack, I stopped. He then said, "Man I understand how you feel. I would've done the same thing if it had been my sister." Then I really felt like an idiot, beating a boy who wasn't putting up any defense. But he never bothered my sister again.

During the latter part of my second year in high school, I discovered sex. Well not really sex, but my hormones had kicked in. Now this was a very difficult time for me because of my Christian upbringing. Church teaching at that time decreed that sex before marriage was a sin. And I went to church every Sunday. Therefore this message was reinforced over and over

But one day, some boys in the higher grades told me about masturbating. Jacking off was the way they described it. When I had a hard on, (an erection), and that was often. I would go to the bathroom to jack off. Now at night after going to bed, was a perfect time for self-gratification. And I took advantage of every opportunity. This worked great for a while, but it became grossly unfulfilling. But it would be quite a long time before I would lose my virginity.

One day I finally had a chance to make out. After watching the older boys make out on the bus while going back and fourth to football and basketball games, my mind was full of fantasies.

So I jumped at this opportunity to make out. And also by this time, I was desperate for female company. The girl's name was Danielle. We were in church at choir rehearsal. And after rehearsal was over, Danielle and I stayed behind. We started necking and things got pretty hot. But there was no sex involved. While this was happening, it was certainly enjoyable. But when it was over, oh did I feel terrible. Disrespecting the House of God and forgetting my religious teaching, I had committed an unforgivable sin. For this I prayed to God everyday for the next six months, asking his forgiveness. Although being God fearing, I didn't think of myself as religious. But I thought God would strike me dead for disrespecting his house. Well it was great making out with her, because I hadn't had this experience before. But I never disrespected the church in this manner again.

In the second year of my high school career, many issues came to the forefront. Where did babies come from? How babies were conceived, racism, and other issues? I was overwhelmed with all of this.

I had little self-esteem, no real ambition, and no real place in the world. And now, moral and social issues had to be dealt with. But I chose not to deal with most of those issues because they had no direct bearing on me. I was really naïve. When told where babies came from, I didn't believe it. How could babies past through such a small canal? The other kids called me dumb. But up to this point, no one had talked to me about the "Birds and the Bees."

I lived in a very small world that consisted basically of my own community. Some might call it a sheltered life. I was oblivious to events happening in other parts of the world.

But I understood racial hatred. After hearing about Emmitt Till, the twelve- year old boy lynched in Mississippi in the middle fifties for speaking to or whistling at a white woman, I retreated farther into my own small world and remained there because it was a safe haven. The balance of my sophomore year passed uneventfully.

My junior year in high school began on an up note. I finally had a girlfriend. Her name was Helen Moss. We actually met in the tenth grade. But things came together my junior year, with the help of my cousin Clint. I told him Helen was pretty cute. He then relayed this message to her and she seemed interested. Thus, a relationship was born.

We were both misfits in school and in our respected communities. I guess this drew us together. She was my girlfriend throughout the rest of high school and the first year of college. Now all during this time, I only kissed her twice. Therefore sex was out of the question. Girls were taught to withhold sex from boys until married. In my world, if a girl gave in to a boy sexually, she was doing him a favor. Girls knew this and would have boys doing all sorts of ridiculous things by promising them sex. Well Helen and I never got that far. And this was beyond me anyway. My mentality about the whole sexual issue was quite different. I was a teenager with the sexual knowledge of an eight year old.

We really never spent much time together. I went to see her one night in my father's junk truck. Arriving about eight o'clock p.m., her stepfather, Mr. Johnson, ordered me to leave at eight fifteen p.m. Now as I went to get into the truck, he ordered me to leave it also. So I had to wait until he was asleep to slip back and drive my truck away. This man made me afraid to visit Helen. He was a huge person.

And I believe Helen and her mother were afraid of him. She never had company from any other friends or classmates and Mr. Johnson had this awful disdain for me. But I believe he had disdain for the world.

I went to see Helen one Wednesday evening. As I drove into the yard, her stepfather ordered me to leave. So I turned around and drove back home. Another evening, my cousin drove me to see Helen. It was about seven p.m. when I arrived and he was instructed to pick me up at ten o clock p.m. Then about eight-thirty, her stepfather ordered me to leave. Since my cousin was to pick me up at ten, I sat on the side of the road until he arrived. With so many obstacles thrown in our path, we really never had a chance for a meaningful relationship. But I tried continually because Helen was a really nice person.

Also during my junior year in high school, I continued in scouting, played in the band, sang in the chorus, played football, and remained the basketball trainer. In addition to working with my father on the junk truck, working as a gardener, and caddying, my time was all accounted for.

Life was bearable because I stayed busy. Being involved in many activities enabled me to focus away from my main problems of stuttering and social acceptance. I spent more time on my schoolwork and was considered academically fairly bright.

The basketball goal in my yard became more important at this time in my life. I lived on the Eastside of town. So the boys from the Westside would come over to play basketball. They were taller and had more basketball skills. The Eastside was constantly beaten by the West. So I organized a basketball tournament between the two sides. This would become an annual event.

Now my organizational skills were beginning to blossom. I somehow became captain for the Eastside, but to this day cannot remember why.

My team could not defeat their team. So I devised a scheme to give us a chance to win. Since they were taller and more skilled, I proposed that we should hold onto the ball, spread the team to the corners, and slow the game down. This accomplished several things. It tried their patience, gave us the element for a surprise attack, and made every basket a premium.

When a scheme like this is employed, the more skillful team is likely to deviate from its game plan. This is exactly what the inferior team wants. The plan worked to perfection. It was called the slowdown tactic. Well the Eastside won the initial basketball tournament and the next two, while I was captain.

Some years later, a now famous coach invented this tactic called the Four Corners Offense. This is the same scheme employed by me as captain of the Eastside team. While not claiming the credit for this invention, I never the less thought of it.

Whenever we played games in which strategy was called for, the teammates looked to me for the answers. I was becoming a person who could think. This capacity increased as the years went by. However, my stuttering and social problems continued.

The summer came and Clint and I went to New Jersey to visit our uncle Early James. We had always imagined he lived in this great big house with a picket fence. When visiting us in the south, Uncle Early James gave the impression that he was rich. Flashing money around and talking like a man of the World, was very natural for him. Well maybe my cousin and I had an over active imaginations. But upon arriving at his home in New Jersey, we were disappointed. Not that his house was not adequate or anything of this nature, it was an ordinary home. It was much like our homes in the south. But we were very impressionable boys.

While in New Jersey, we met many young girls. Well we were at least acquainted with them. But all we did was to walk by these girls and smile. We knew nothing about flirting.

I met a really pretty girl named Wilhelmena. She was to be my new girlfriend. Well this was mostly in my mind, but somehow I believed it. So for the next few years, I carried a torch in my heart for a girl I hardly knew. During this time, I spoke maybe ten words in total to her. Now that really took imagination. But it sustained me for quite a few years.

Uncle Early James was a very nice man and made us feel very comfortable in his home. We met many of our northern family members and this was quite a thrill. Clint and I really enjoyed our trip to the North. But when we left for home, I was still a virgin and wasn't any closer to changing that status than before. Now it was back home to the ridicule of my friends, to the basketball goal in my yard, and to my ever- present social problems.

But during this year, there were other changes in my life. I learned to dance, well, at least the Cha Cha. In my community, I became the

Cha Cha champion. Nobody had my steps or my moves. I could really do it.

Now in Jonesboro where I lived, there was a café called Mauddy Bee's. So on Wednesday and Saturday nights, we met at Mauddy Bee's to dance. These were called Canteen Nights. Everybody around my age would come. There were boys and girls from Hapeville Georgia, just east of the Atlanta Airport. Girls and boys from Forest Park Georgia also came. Forest Park is where we all went to school. Therefore we knew almost everybody there. Since Mauddy Bee's cafe was in Jonesboro, then of course the kids from this community showed up.

These canteen nights were well attended. And we had a really great time profiling and trying to be cool in addition to dancing. There was the occasional fight when one group disrespected the other. Things happened but we weren't as violent, nor did we fight to the death of the other person. But on those nights, each boy and girl came dressed in his or her coolest outfit. The finest girls were the talk of the boys. And of course the coolest boys were the talk of the girls. Since I was not considered cool, that left me out.

This was like a scene from an earlier version of "Saturday Night Fever." We danced and sweated until about twelve o'clock a.m. Most boys loved the slow records so they could dance really close to the girls. This bumping and grinding was a lot of fun.

Many boys would end up with a hard on (erection), but this was part of the fun process. When this happened, the girls would laugh because boys had to extend their hand down in front of their groin area to hide an obvious hard on. But everyone knew what was happening.

If I was lucky enough to get a hard on, then my evening at the canteen was a success. Sometime boys and girls would disappear for a short period of time to score. But this never happened in my case.

Ruth Harris and Joan Daley were the finest and most admired girls in my age group. They were the "Prima Donna's" of the day, and all the girls in our age group were measured against them. Dancing with or being seen with either of these girls was what the boys dreamed of. They were our fantasy, and remained the standard throughout high school.

But at the dances, I was a wallflower. And it was mostly my fault because I was afraid to ask girls to dance. Being a boy of low self-esteem, I was very fearful of rejection. But when a Cha Cha record was played, I sprang into action. I was reborn and transformed into a dancing machine. My partner was, yes, Joan Daley. We were the best team of Cha Cha dancers for miles around. Our favorite record was "Dianna," by Paul Anka.

So when this record played, the other people let us have the floor. Wow! This was really fun. And I felt like someone special, while dancing with Joan.

However, I didn't get the girl. Now back as a wallflower after my favorite dance, I observed the cool people, while trying to be cool myself. Occasionally, I would have the opportunity to slow drag with a girl. And of course I would get a hard on. This embarrassed me greatly and I would again retreat to the sidelines.

Most kids stuck with their group and hung together. But even with my lack of social acceptance, Canteen Nights were still special. I could fantasize about being with the girls, and being cool like the other boys.

This café was a hub of activity for the entire community. We could stop by for a snack, play pool, or just hang out and talk. This was the place, the only place in town for this purpose.

Miss Mauddy Bee, as we called her, was an older woman. She was the grandmother of Fred Robinson, a member of my Doo Wop group. But this café was her life, and she made lots of money from it.

The Canteen and all activity surrounding it played a pivotal role in my development. This scene would repeat itself throughout my high school career and I continued to hone my Cha Cha skills there. In reflection, those were some of my most enjoyable times. I will never forget Mauddy Bee's.

Ruth and Joan continued to be the finest and most admired girls in my class, according to the boys, for the rest of our high school days.

Now having a girlfriend like Ruth and Joan was out of the question for me. My peers had always spoken of me in such negative terms and with such regularity until I believed what they said. With my low self-esteem, I couldn't fathom having a relationship with these girls. So I didn't think that I deserved either of them. But in retrospect, they were pretty normal girls. In our past or present, there were and still are peers we think are unreachable.

I said to myself many time, there will be a rebirth that will transform me into an acceptable human being. So I prayed, change please hurry. I am sinking fast and will drown in an ocean of doubt and low self-esteem. But until the change happens, help me to find a way to endure and survive.

My peers didn't dislike me for myself. But my circumstances were unfortunate. When peers don't understand certain problems, they often respond by making fun of the affected person. They on many occasions can be very cruel. My peers were cruel sometimes without knowing it. However this didn't help my circumstances. But some days my peer group and I acted like normal teenagers, exploring many facets of our lives. Much of this was fascinating even to me.

But again while this was happening, I continued telling myself that things would change in the future. This was my survival plea. My acceptance as a human being would take place in this lifetime. I had to keep the faith at all cost.

My senior year in high school was beginning and many issues confronted me. Graduation, the Senior Prom, money for senior activities, and thoughts of what to do with my life, were just a few. The fear of uncharted territory loomed heavily in my mind. High school up to this point, hadn't prepared me to do anything career wise. And in the Deep South during this period, there were no jobs for unskilled black men. Even the skilled black men had difficulty in the work force.

In examining the academic departments of my high school, most were lacking in content. There was no real chemistry department and no foreign language department at all. The English department was probably adequate, but the Math department was grossly inadequate. Home economics was mandatory for all students to graduate. And this course actually helped me.

Two requirements needed to pass home economics were, to make a garment and make or create a food item. So I secured a pattern and made a shirt which turned out very well, and I was very proud of it. Next, Ma gave me a recipe for cookies, and I made them. They were fantastic. Later, the students presented a fashion show for their parents. Here they could sample food cooked by the students, and see garments made and modeled by the students. This was a fun time for teachers, parents, and students.

Well being an entertainer of sorts, I sang several songs at this event. Most of them were Hillbilly pieces. So in the midst of what the school wasn't doing, it was socializing us. And I suppose that was important. The teachers did the best job possible with the meager resources available.

But there was no college preparation because I wasn't going. In fact, it had never entered my mind. My family was extremely poor and couldn't afford to send me. So this was an open and shut case. Since I already knew this, it didn't bother me. But being in this world with no place to go or nothing to do certainly did bother me.

So I continued on the path set by me before. That was just going with the flow and not making any waves. I went to school, played in the band, sang in the chorus and generally stayed on top of my studies. There were no real ambitions in my thought process at this time.

After having several talks with Mrs. Thomas, a social studies teacher, about life and where we fit into it, I suddenly began to dream of another world, a better world for me.

It was a world in which I would become a success. But this world, I would probably never see. So during the balance of the year, I was very uncomfortable living in a state of flux and uncertainty.

I certainly had a good year on the gridiron. My agility was very good, instincts were above average, made good decisions, and was the quickest player on the team. But I wasn't taken seriously. My weight was one hundred twenty five pounds. So in the coach's minds, how far could a player of this size go? So I was overlooked when it came to athletic superlatives and awards. But I believed deep in my heart, I was good enough to play for many college teams. Another super athlete, named Joe Bert Mitchell, would claim most of the awards. He deserved them, but I just felt left out.

I worked overtime as a gardener and as a caddy to pay my senior dues. The class ring was purchased, my graduation robe was rented, my yearbook was purchased, the class picnic was paid for, and my contribution toward a gift for our homeroom teacher was taken care of. So plans leading up to my graduation were on schedule.

It was decided that the yearbook content would include all class superlatives. Well there was not one for me. I wasn't the most likely to succeed, wasn't the most handsome boy, wasn't the best dressed, wasn't the best athlete, and none of the other class superlatives.

But one class member stepped up and said, "We must find something for Turnipseed." So, another class member came up with this bright idea. "Let's name him the most studious boy." In those days, this was an insult because it had nerdy connotations. Imagine, even when my classmates were trying to appease me, they came up with an insult. Well insults were nothing new to me. So I just took it all in stride.

My girlfriend Helen was named Valedictorian of our high school graduating class. I was particularly proud of her. And we celebrated by having a soda together at a local diner. Her stepfather wouldn't give us permission to do anything else

But the senior prom was approaching and she was to be my date. I didn't have a car, but arrangements were made to pick her up for this last great school event before graduation. My blue suit had been pressed and I was going to purchase a corsage for her dress. We both looked forward to this event because it was to be our first significant date. She looked extremely radiant in the days leading up to the prom, and I was happier than I had been in a long time.

But about a week before the prom, Helen informed me that she wouldn't be unable to attend. The both of us were devastated. Mr. Johnson had forbidden Helen from going to the prom with me and to attend at all. The only high school senior prom I would ever have, and my best girl couldn't attend. I was in a fog and decided not to go either. But Helen encouraged me to go to the prom.

For the very first time, I saw pain in her eyes. This made me realize what tremendous pressure she had to live under from her stepfather. From this point, my compassion and respect for her grew tremendously. I will never forget the hurt and pain we endured in connection with this disappointment.

But now I had to come up with another date. There was a friend who had a sister. And this is the person I took on the most important date of my life. So for my senior prom, I had a blind date. She was a girl I hadn't laid eyes on before. This was a traumatic experience as well as a drag. All my life, I looked forward to the prom. And ending up with a blind date was a disaster.

Her name was Annie Jean. And she was actually very pretty. But we had nothing in common. From the first moment we met, there was apprehension on both of our parts. I gave her a corsage which didn't match her dress. And during the evening, we didn't dance very much. We just sat around and watched each other. The evening moved slowly and was quite painful. I was cordial in getting punch for her. And we both really tried to make this as pleasant as possible, but it was impossible.

When the prom was finally over, I took her home. And there were no after parties. I would only see Annie Jean on two other occasions in my whole life. But I wondered how she felt and what she thought of the whole situation. Well I never found out. And she later married Ward, a member of my Doo Wop singing group.

Now graduation was upon us. Last minute preparations were in progress. "Pomp and Circumstance" was the standard graduation marching music for our school. And we practiced marching in and out of the assembly hall religiously. I loved that music and still do.

Boys wore dark suits and girls white dresses. Graduation was a very stately affair at that time. My parents were very proud because I was the first high school graduate in the family.

Well graduation came and it was a great day. Helen gave the valedictorian address. And it was very good. I played in the school's band and sang in the chorus for the last time. It was sort of sad in a way. Most of the parties and celebrations had taken place. We bade our teachers so long and most of us were on our way into the unknown. To me, graduation was a tremendous let down.

But I suppose it was that way for many of the other students. There was an awful empty feeling in the pit of my stomach when I graduated and realized I had nothing to look forward to and no place to go. Armed with a diploma, but with no skills, then being sent out into the world to survive was indeed very scary.

During my life many crises had arisen. And I had endured them all. But in my mind, the greatest crisis was beginning now. There were things in my life that made me very proud. With all the problems encountered, whether social, financial, or educational, I didn't develop anger toward the world, my parents, or my peers. I didn't feel sorry for myself, or feel that the world owed me anything.

Ma taught me at an early age, that one of the most destructive emotions was anger. I learned that anger could destroy me and also cause me to destroy others. It could keep me from developing my full potential. Ma said, "I should develop more positive instincts." It was very difficult to think positively at this time. I wasn't angry, just sad. But my whole life lay ahead, and I had to develop some direction.

THE COLLEGE YEARS

Postgraduate depression had begun to creep into my life. I was in a state of flux, with nothing positive happening at this point.

Then a wonderful person, who would become my mentor and savior, came into my life. Her name was Eula V. Arnold. Actually, I had known her all my life. She was quite civic minded and was a very prominent person in the city of Jonesboro, Georgia.

One day I was summoned to her home. Upon entering, she asked this question, "What are you going to do with your life boy?" My reply was, "I have no clue." We talked for a while and I explained that my family was not in a position financially to send me to college. Since this was the case, and I knew it to be true, I had not applied to any college.

After explaining the situation to her, she began to write a letter. When it was finished, Miss Arnold sealed it, gave it to me, and said. "Take this letter up to Clark College in Atlanta and give it to the president." I was sort of puzzled because she meant the president of the college.

I didn't know what was going to happen. But I obeyed as always, when it came to Miss Arnold. So I called the college immediately to arrange an appointment

I arrived at Clark College about eight o'clock a. m. the next morning for my scheduled appointment with the president. He had no idea what I was there for. So I gave him the letter. He seemed puzzled. But he read the letter

A smile began to appear on his face and he said, "oh, Miss Arnold." I didn't know what that meant. Then he said. "Go down stairs and register."

My mind was blown. Register for what, I asked? You are going to be a student at Clark College, the president replied. Miss Arnold is going to be your sponsor and will make all provisions for you. I sat there for a few minutes in a state of shock. Was I dreaming, a college student? The President shook my hand. This awakened me slightly, and he took my arm and escorted me down to the registrar's office. I couldn't have made it on my own. Walking down the stairs to register, I was not of this world. Floating on clouds was more like it. Now reaching the register, I had to sit down and pinch myself. This all seemed like a fairy tale. In a matter of minutes, my life had been changed forever. Wow this was unbelievable.

I couldn't wait to get home and share the great news with Ma and Da-Cliff. They were waiting for me with anticipation. I learned that Miss Arnold had discussed this with them before hand, to get their approval. But I knew nothing of it.

Now Ma and Da-Cliff were extremely proud and happy. Not only was I the first family member to finish high school, but now a college student. The whole family, immediate and extended, plus many friends, came to our house that weekend to help us celebrate.

To become an official college student, I had to submit an application for admission. This was done a few days later. And I remember this being quite an exciting day.

Later I learned Miss Arnold was a classmate, while in college, of the president of Clark College. But more importantly, she was a huge contributor financially, to Clark College. The contents of the letter had me very curious. But I didn't question Miss Arnold.

Suddenly from nothing to do, and no place to go, being reborn. This was the most amazing development in my young life. Wow!!! Maybe my prayers were being answered. Maybe the rebirth was beginning.

Maybe I was going to be a person, a productive human being after all. Yes, I pondered my future. Yes, many obstacles lay ahead. But for the time being, my future looked a great deal more promising. But I still found those developments very hard to believe.

Helen was also accepted as a student at Clark College. And I believed from this point, we would actually have a chance to develop our relationship. But it wasn't meant to be because we couldn't get it together. We tried, but our lives were going in different directions. She remained at Clark for a year and a half. After that, she dropped out. And I have not seen or heard from her since.

From when I was very young, the belief that God had something planned for me lingered in the back of my mind. My humble beginning, financial status, lack of educational opportunities, social non-acceptance, speech impediment, and now a miracle college student, was the emergence of something good and noble.

Maybe another Dr. King, a Dr. E. Franklin Frazier, a Jackie Robinson, a George Washington Carver, a Nat Cole, or even a Malcolm X., were prominent people who I might emulate. Well my imagination was working overtime.

Now college lay before me. So my world leadership would have to wait. I had survived many trials and tribulations, but college would become my greatest challenge.

Freshman year

College was supposed to be the beginning, the rebirth of Al Turnipseed. But when I arrived, it seemed like the death of Al Turnipseed, talk about culture shock. And soon learning that I knew absolutely nothing was difficult to say the least.

In high school, I was academically pretty bright. But college was another world, and it threw me for a loop. It seemed like I had been thrown into a river with twenty-foot waves, with no conception of how to swim. I was in way over my head.

My first instinct was to go home. In my mind, I didn't belong in college. Deep depression was slowly overtaking me.

But somehow, I had to hold it together. If I gave up so soon, my family would be very disappointed.

Meeting with the counselors during the placement interviews, only heightened my anxiety. Questions were asked like, "What will be your major?" My reply, "what is a major"? What foreign language did you take in high school? "How much math and chemistry have you had?" These questions startled me.

In high school, I had no counseling or college preparatory information, and I didn't know what a major was. Talking about another language was as foreign as the language itself. And my chemistry and math were inadequate.

The counselor explained that a major is your field of study, while in college. Well I couldn't name a major. Then a great question was asked by the counselor, "What do you like?" My reply was "Music." Thus, my major became music.

I often reflect on the process of choosing what I would do for the balance of my life. It could've very well been English, social studies or anything. But the way I chose my major, was not very sound at all. A better thought process should've prevailed. But I didn't know. I was lost.

I wouldn't recommend this process to anyone who is undecided about a major in college. In hindsight, I probably should've majored in business. It was more adaptable.

But I don't regret studying music. It changed my whole life. As it turned out, I knew absolutely nothing about music either. So I started from scratch. Well I could read music.

In my first year, ear training and sight singing were a real challenge to my music education. With the extra stress caused by this difficult major, my self-esteem plummeted even more, and my stuttering persisted.

The College Years

I received a band music scholarship of one hundred dollars. And it seemed like a lot at the time. So I went to audition for the band. The band director mentioned A, B, and C music. So I asked, "What is "A music?" A music is the most difficult to play, B and C graduates downward, he explained

In my high school background, C music was all I knew. And in high school, I was considered a good French horn player. Well after listening to the great instrumentalists during the audition, I wasn't in the same league with any of them. So I quickly and quietly packed up my instrument, left the audition, and never returned.

This was another major blow in my rude awakening. The disdain for my high school and its teachers overflowed. They had set me up for failure. They had lied to me. What I was taught in high school didn't prepare me for college at all. But after thinking about this situation for a while, my high school teachers probably did the best job they could've under adverse conditions.

When the band started to rehearse, I just went into the band room and rehearsed also. From that point, I played in the college marching band and the orchestra until graduation. When music classes started, I just went in the door.

I went to a predominantly black college and it helped rescue me and a lot of black students. So there are a few things I must say about the predominantly black colleges at that time, and the reasons I think these colleges were so valuable to the black community. It provided an opportunity for people of color, who otherwise had no chance for an education.

Their philosophy included these thoughts. As a high school student, you may not have come from the best educational situation. Maybe your SAT scores wouldn't qualify for Harvard or Yale and many other colleges. But we (the black colleges) think you have the IQ. So we want to give you (students) the opportunity to receive an education and to become productive members of this society.

I understood that some students could qualify for Harvard and Yale, but couldn't afford to attend. Again, up stepped the black colleges.

I will always respect and love these predominantly black colleges for giving people like me the opportunity for an education in a world where we might have been educationally trampled. This philosophy was relayed to me during a freshman orientation lecture.

Being a college student had become the most dominating and difficult time in my life. I was expected to learn about the world, how to exist globally, and how to support myself. But knowing I wasn't ready to tackle these issues, made this time very scary. I just didn't believe that I could survive in college. It was too difficult.

I had a heart to heart talk with Miss Arnold. She explained that my symptoms were those of many college students. I just had to hang in there and give it more time. Miss Arnold had a way of making things seem so much better.

So I must confess, after speaking with her, things looked a little brighter. Maybe I just needed a shoulder to cry on or just sympathy. Well Miss Arnold provided both.

But to survive in college, I had to learn other skills. In the early years I simply stayed out of people's way, to be anonymous, to be in the background. But in college, it was different. My social patterns had to change. I had to be more mature, and had to learn how to manage my time better.

Friends to help me adjust socially, was a must. I had none. Using the library and reference books were foreign to me. In high school, since we needed more classroom space, the library was used for this purpose. But in college, the library was most important for study.

I didn't read the newspaper. My family did not have a television during my adolescence. My world had been wrapped up in the local community where I lived. Therefore many world events were unknown to me. The Korean War, World War Two, the World Series, and normal things that other students were exposed to prior to college, were foreign to me. So in addition to college academics, I had to learn normal things.

It was like rowing a boat against the tide. And the roughest water was still ahead. I didn't know what my breaking point was. But it was getting closer.

Another talk with Miss Arnold calmed my fears for the moment. She said. "The world is a tough place to live in sometimes, but you must be tough all the time." A pep talk is what I needed and it regenerated me for the moment. Miss Arnold was right again.

I learned a new survival skill. I removed myself emotionally and mentally from painful situations. When this type of situation cropped up, I wouldn't acknowledge that pain was there. It hardened me and I could cope.

Now in many ways this wasn't good, because being a hardened person, my ability to feel was compromised. When people thought I was having a very difficult time, I was just dead on the inside, and the difficulty was numbed. I never cried about anything again. I developed a much tougher skin.

My academic load was very heavy. It consisted of eighteen hours or credits for the first semester. It was a very large load since the average was twelve to fourteen credits per semester. I took remedial math and English courses designed to bring me up to speed in college math and English. I took a French course for beginners. These courses were taken in addition to the regular curriculum for college freshmen. Since the courses were designed to bring students up to speed, there were no academic credits given for them. Yes, this was really a struggle.

I learned to take accurate notes during lecture courses. And time was a premium. Most courses other freshman took for granted were a struggle to me. But so were most other college activities.

As a band member, I took the music home to study over and over. Notes taken during lectures were carefully studied also. For me, extra study became a way of life. I truly lived on the edge of panic.

My college existence became a day to day process. There were no long range plans in my mind at all. I couldn't see myself lasting for even an entire week.

So it was reduced to the lowest denominator, one day at a time. These days dragged on and on. But they became weeks and weeks became months and somehow I finished the first year.

But while struggling through my freshman year, strange things were happening. Many students who were much better prepared than I were dropping by the wayside. I thought this was ironic. So I kept going.

The grade average for my first year was about a C+. Most of my student friends didn't consider this very good. But to me, it was a miracle that I survived. Miss Arnold was very happy for me. But I didn't feel that way. These were the lowest grades I had ever received in my entire life. Since I had persevered, this is what I was most proud of.

For the summer, my uncle Early James had secured a job for me in New Jersey. And I was very happy to get away from home and my father's junk truck. But this job turned out to be not much better.

I worked in a foundry where cast iron moldings were made for business and industry. This job frightened me very much. I was working around hot molting iron ore all day. To me it was like working in a volcano. It was always hot, smoky, and dangerous. Breathing in the acid laced smoke was not good for my health either.

Three other uncles, who all worked at this foundry, later died from cancer. Many others did also. So I knew this wasn't the place for me. But I did stay for the summer.

I met a few girls, but nothing really happened. Socializing with girls was quite stressful since my stuttering was still quite severe. So I continued to live within myself. My focus was on trying to accumulate money for the upcoming school year.

I purchased Clothes for the next year from my summer earnings. But not much money was saved otherwise. My salary was very low, but I was learning to be more independent. The summer was about over, so I said goodbye to my New Jersey relatives and returned homes.

The pressure and the anxiety I had felt, during my freshman year, was returning. Another year of pain and suffering was about to begin.

Sophomore year

During this year, I was expected to take more courses in my major field of study. Since music was my major, I met with the head of the department to map out my future class schedule.

The department head was Dr. J.deKoven Killingsworth. We would have, for the next three years, a cordial relationship. He was also the chorus director and I became a member. It was called The Philharmonic Society. Now being a member of this chorus, was a really great experience.

I wasn't one of Dr. Killingsworth's favorite chorus members. And to this day, I don't know why. Well I am not saying that he disliked me. Now I was a member of the bass section.

While not being the best bass singer in the section, I was very conscious of pitch and often kept the entire section together and on pitch. My music ear was always very good. Dr. Killingsworth depended on me for this.

But I wasn't selected as a member of the traveling chorus. The Philharmonic Society was presented in a concert, in my hometown of Jonesboro, sponsored by Miss Arnold. This was the one and only time I traveled with the chorus. From the school campus, we took a bus to Jonesboro. I could've met them there. But Dr. Killingsworth wanted to show the people of Jonesboro, that I was in the chorus. Therefore he insisted that I ride the bus with the others members. This made my mother feel proud, and it also made me feel good. But this was my only time traveling with the chorus, to any concert, outside the college's domain.

During my tenure at Clark, I supported Dr. Killingsworth in all his endeavors. Whatever he asked me to do, I complied. His favorite students didn't do this at all. And when he died, many years later, I attended his funeral. Not one of his favorite students attended. But again, we had no major problems while I attended college, and we continued to work together.

Wayman Carver was also a significant instructor during my college days. He was the director of the college marching and concert bands. I was member of both. He didn't consider me one of his favorites either. Since I wasn't a great horn player, maybe he didn't think I belonged in music. But he depended on me to play in both bands. So up to this point, I wasn't anyone's favorite, and really didn't need to be.

I just needed someone at Clark to be in my corner. But neither Dr. Killingsworth's nor Mr. Carver's attitude did anything for my confidence.

But I had to continue my journey just the same. In the music department, I worked with Mr. Carver for the balance of my college career. I took many music related courses from him. And yes, I passed them all.

During this year, many changes were to take place within me. I took a course in English Literature with an instructor named Dr. Jackson. Well my grade wasn't very good. But I began to learn about the world of literature. She introduced me to Greek Tragedies and to Shakespeare. Wow, this was a whole new world and I was fascinated. Suddenly, elements in the world began to take on a different order. I understood how the world of the past related to the present. I would read great literary works for hours each day. My thirst was unquenchable. Many questions, both moral and social, that had plagued me during most of my life were suddenly answered and made clearer through literature. Reading Antigone was particularly very interesting to me.

After all this, I barely received a passing grade. Dr. Jackson explained that I had to expand my horizons. She put her thumb and index fingers together forming a small circle and said. "You live in a world about this size. Maybe one day you will break out and discover there is a big wide world to explore." This had a profound affect on me and fueled an atmosphere for new discovery. But I still believe she was unfair with the grade.

The College Years

I took a course in intermediate French, and was doing very well with a B+ average. My French instructor, named Ms. Grover, summoned me to her office. I arrived and immediately sat in a chair directly across from her. She had on a very short dress and began crossing and uncrossing her legs in front of me. Her dress was sliding upward and I was very nervous. Of course I was aware of the situation. But my training and upbringing said "Don't look."

She asked me to come to her apartment for further help in French. And I said to her amazement, "I don't need any help in French." "My average is a B+." My reply shocked her and she asked me to leave her office.

My finale grade was a big fat "C." Now I was in shock. How could this be? A football player Named Tony Mandy, who didn't know the first thing about French, and rarely attended the sessions, received an "A" in the very same class.

I was livid and really couldn't understand what was happening. One of my classmates eventually explained the situation to me. He said that I was the most ignorant, naïve, and stupid person alive. Well actually I was. And I just wasn't familiar with some aspects in the world of discovery and exploration.

Since Ms. Grover never spoke to me again during my college career, I never got a second chance to discover more about French with her. I thought about this incident many times after it happened. It was not my time, and maybe it was a learning experience.

To my chagrin, many more unrequited experiences were in store for me. During the year, there were two girls I sort of liked. Now I was still shy and naïve, but was trying. They looked at me with those inquisitive smiles, and I had the impression that maybe there was a chance for me to finally start a relationship with one of these girls. But I found out later, they were both having an affair with the same professor.

Now I was beginning to think this would never happen for me. Maybe girls just didn't like me. After all I was a social misfit with a stuttering problem. Maybe I wasn't good enough.

One day I approached my old girlfriend Helen. And in a kidding manner, asked her to go to a local motel with me. To my surprise, she said "yes." I thought she was kidding. So we began to walk toward the motel. I was waiting for her to say, changed my mind. And this would give me a chance to gracefully bow out.

Well she didn't change her mind and I was in a panic situation. Not that I was afraid to go with her, I had no money. So arriving in front of the motel, I said sheepishly. "I have no money for the motel." To say that she was angry would be an understatement. Helen was livid, not because of the money, but because I had her walk all the way to the motel knowing the situation.

It seemed whenever this type of opportunity presented itself, I wasn't up to the challenge. I was still a virgin with no prospects on the horizon.

For the first semester of my sophomore year, I had decent grades. My thoughts were, maybe I am college material after all. Since my grades were good, a fraternity recruited me. I pledged to join The Omega Psi Phi Fraternity. Now during the pledge period, there were a lot of hazing, many beatings, meaningless chores, and just embarrassing incidents. One day the pledges for the Omega Fraternity had to bathe in garlic, and get dressed in tuxedos. Everyone thought we looked great. But as we were approached, they ran for cover.

This was perhaps the beginning of my socialization. Using the fraternity as a base, I was invited to more parties, met more people, participated in more activities, and was generally accepted more favorably. For the first time in my life, I had a feeling of belonging. Well this fraternity was the most popular organization on campus. So I was accepted at face value, as a result of being a member.

It became my family. Dr. Killingsworth and Mr. Carver were also members. So during the college years, and in my later life, I met many prominent members of the Omega Fraternity from across the nation.

Since I was a Music Major, professor Killingsworth decided to give me a part in a Chinese Opera called Bow Sing that was presented by the music department. I was very excited. Then he said, "You have only one line." Well my rationale was I still have a part in the opera. So I accepted the part.

This proved to be a very difficult role for me. The reasons were different than I perceived.

I arrived about two hours before each performance for a scheduled appointment with the makeup artist. Imagine, two hours in makeup to look Chinese. Then I appeared on stage during the first scene. In fact, I was the first scene. After singing my one line, "No no Bow Sing he had not passed this way," it was over for me. I could leave and go home.

The opera ran for one full week and was very draining. Two hours in make up, for less than two minutes on stage, caused me to question why I was doing this in the first place.

Well none of my family members and friends was invited, because I wasn't pleased with my part in the opera. If they were two minutes late, my entire performance would be missed. This was some experience and I suppose it was positive.

Grades during my second year in college, improved tremendously. I finally believed that I was worthy of being there. But many problems remained and were magnified.

I still stuttered constantly, lacked self esteem, social problems although somewhat better, still plagued me, and was still a virgin. This one fact made my other problems seem greater.

Now in addition to those issues, I had no money for college necessities, for lunch, for social activities, and for transportation. And I fought depression much of the time. But I managed to complete my second year. But if things didn't change for the next year, I couldn't see myself coping with this same situation. It was a must for me to make changes.

THE MAGNIFICENT GROUP

Before continuing my journey to the next college year, there are a few very important people I must mention. From meeting these people, a better understanding will develop as to how I managed to cope during this most difficult period. Without this group, who virtually saved me, college wouldn't have been possible. I owe my life, my being, my soul, my spirit, my will, and my accomplishments to this magnificent group, who coddled and nurtured me through some of the most turbulent times of my life.

In order for a team to succeed, there must be cooperation and help from others and other sources. Likewise in my triumph, changing from a non-person into a productive human being, I had to have help from others. As long as I live, the soul and the spirit of these seven people are etched into my very being.

Eula V. Arnold is foremost on this list. She is the first person who recognized that maybe I was worth rescuing. Doors began to open when Miss Arnold, as we called her, suggested that I deliver a letter, written by her, to the president of Clark College.

I learned later this letter stated, "This will introduce Alfred Turnipseed, a boy who needs a chance. He has an inquisitive mind, good values, good qualities, and a great spirit.

These traits must be cultivated. He needs a chance. Don't worry about the money. I am prepared to take a risk along with him, because

I believe he is worth it. Please give him the opportunity. This letter was signed Eula Arnold. When told of the contents of this letter, chills ran up and down my spine. She wrote this letter while talking to me in her home. What did she see in me?

She suggested that I take a chance on going to college. Well Miss Arnold, a community philanthropist, made provisions for me to attend Clark College in Atlanta, Georgia. She provided most of the financial support, and offered emotional support and encouragement.

Many times I wanted to just throw in the towel, but she wouldn't let me. After our weekly heart to heart talks, Miss Arnold would pray and then remind me that she recognized certain qualities and traits in me worthy of cultivating. I never knew what these traits were.

Miss Arnold was a community organizer, an educator, a Sunday school teacher, a Bible School teacher, a church school pianist, a mentor, a friend and humanitarian to the people of Jonesboro, and to the world. And I will always love Miss Arnold. I owe my life to this wonderful person. Without her, I might have fallen through the cracks of society and never recovered. She was gentle, kind, loving, intelligent, and tenacious.

As a pianist for the Sunday school, she couldn't play at all. But she always continued and never wavered. We would be singing in one key and she would suddenly play in another. But even this didn't embarrass her. She just kept playing and smiling.

During the holidays, she would organize plays and sing-a-longs for the community. The definition of the word "Saint" is Miss Arnold. She never married. So her lifetime was spent helping people like me, who otherwise had no other chance at a better life. This is what gave her saintly qualities.

She was a very stately woman about five feet seven inches tall. Never one to wear makeup, she wore glasses and plain print dresses. In all the years associating with Miss Arnold, I never once heard a negative word come out of her mouth.

She really commanded respect. Even alcoholics in the streets straightened up as she walked by. They would greet her by saying,

"Hello Miss Arnold." She would simply smile and tell them to come to church.

Although she was willing to give her support to any person in the community, most people believed I was her favorite. I wasn't really, but her advice to me was followed without questions and unconditionally. My question to her was, "How will I ever be able to repay you?" Her reply was, "I don't want you to repay me." "Just be a good citizen and try to help another person achieve in the manner I am helping you." "This will be enough compensation for me." Tears came to my eyes when she told me this. I learned much about humility from Miss Arnold.

Money was needed for books, tuition, and other school supplies. Miss Arnold would ask me, "What do you need and how much does it cost?" She would give me a check for whatever the cost was. She never questioned the amount or complained about it. This was a four year commitment and Miss Arnold paid and kept me on track for the entire time.

Since I felt guilty accepting this aid from her, something had to be done on my part to justify it. So I became her gardener. I cut her grass, kept her car clean, and ran errands for her. She let me know this was not required for her to help me. So at my request, Miss Arnold allowed me to keep my pride by agreeing to let me do this.

In my quest to become a good productive citizen and a good person, I have never forgotten what Miss Arnold gave me. She gave me her love, her time, her money, and her emotional support. She was my savior. Her spirit is etched in my heart forever.

I could always seek her counsel on a wide range of matters, whether business, financial, moral, family, or emotional issues. Miss Arnold was my inner strength until the day she died. And I still derive strength from her.

I will speak of the next two persons in terms of one, my mother and father. Ma and Da-Cliff is what I called them. They were extremely important in my development, and in my obtaining a college education.

I recognized early in high school that they couldn't afford to send me to college. But they did encourage me to go with Miss Arnold's financial support. And they were very grateful to Miss Arnold.

Whatever they could do to alleviate some of the pressure during my college years, it was done very happily. Sometimes lunch money, sometimes transportation, and moral support, Ma and Da-Cliff were always there.

I asked Ma one day for five dollars to buy a book for one of my courses. She opened her wallet containing only one dollar and said, "This is all I have, but you can have it." Ma offered me one hundred percent of everything she had. How could anyone top this unselfish act of love? I became very emotional and gave her a big hug. And I also declined to take Ma's last dollar.

Ma and Da-Cliff were very strong-minded and had great faith in me. Without them, I would've given up. What they contributed, I cannot repay. They will forever be a part of me. They are in my heart.

Number four in this group is a cousin of mine by the name of M. T. Star. I never knew what the initials stood for and still don't. But he recognized that I was struggling to go to college. Therefore he decided to help. I suppose he was like an older brother, when I needed one.

But M.T. was also a trusted friend all the time. He offered transportation, found odd jobs for me, and occasionally would buy books or lunch if this were needed.

One night I was returning home on the bus after a long day in school. Well sleep overtook me quickly. I awakened later to discover being about fifty miles from home and in Klu Klux Klan territory. I got off the bus, called M.T., and told him where I was. He got out of bed about eleven o'clock at night and drove fifty miles to pick me up. I couldn't call my home because we had no phone. M.T. strongly suggested that I stay out of sight until he picked me up.

He never complained about having been asked to do this, or any of the many things I would ask him to do during my college days. I could call on him for anything at anytime. I can still do this.

He has a lovely wife named Catherine and three lovely daughters named Linda, Connie, and my favorite Angelia. This is a family that loved me. I knew it then, and I know it now. M.T. said to me one day, that I was the model and the inspiration for his children to pursue a higher education. I love him and his family very much and I am still very close to all of them. M. T. Star remains one of my best and most respected friends.

Barbara Welborn is next in this group of seven. She was my beloved sister who was a rock in terms of her support for me.

During my freshman year, Barbara lived in one tiny room. But she always gave me a pallet for sleeping on the floor, if I wasn't able to go home. As she prospered and her conditions improved, she always shared her living quarters with me at no cost. When I needed food, she also shared what she had with me.

Barbara and I shared a love of music. She was a renowned gospel singer in the Atlanta area. I assisted her on many occasions with her gospel programming and met many of the country's top gospel singers.

But throughout her busy life and busy career, she would always take the time to listen and advise me in many matters. I knew no matter what the situation was my sister would always be there for me. She proved time and time again, that our bond was really strong and that she really loved me.

Barbara never asked for money or anything in return. She was really proud because I was the first member of the family to go to college. To her, this was compensation enough.

She was really a great role model, a great mentor, and a great friend. She remains one of my most trusted relatives and friends. Her goodness will live in my heart always. And I will always love her dearly.

Pal Harris was another member of this group of seven. During my college career, Mr. Harris' occupation brought him close to the college campus. This was perfect for me transportation wise. Therefore he was contracted to take me to the campus every school day. This worked fine until one day, I had no more money. I informed Mr. Harris that I couldn't afford to pay for my transportation any longer. He replied, "I will pick you up tomorrow." He asked. "Do you think I am going to let you down now?" Don't worry about the money. He further explained. This was his way of helping me, a struggling student, who obviously wanted to get a college education. I was really touched by this gesture from a man who just wanted to help.

He became one of my great supporters and always seemed to be in my corner. He had a very calm demeanor and this helped me through many tense situations. I will never forget this very kind man.

The last of this special group is Rev. C.L. Henderson. I met him as a teenager. He had come to pastor Andrew Chapel Methodist Church in Jonesboro Ga., my home church. The whole community embraced him because he was personable, kind, and very knowledgeable.

I didn't know at the time of our first meeting, that he was a Clark College graduate. Upon finding out I was going to be a student at Clark, he offered many word of encouragement. He also discovered I didn't have many resources. He certainly did his part in helping me to matriculate and travel back and forth.

On occasions when I had no money for lunch, he would buy it, while telling me not to worry about paying him back. But he also knew I had no way of paying him back at the time. Rev Henderson wanted me to become a productive citizen, as he put it.

But one of the most important things he did, and the other members of this group of seven did, was to keep my spirit up. He continually encouraged me to persevere, to push on, and not give up.

He knew most of the professors at Clark, so his advice was invaluable to me in choosing the right ones for specific courses. He provided spiritual support as well. Rev. Henderson was a singer. While at Clark, he was a member of the Philharmonic Society. So we had music in common. He continued to be a source of support throughout my college career. I thank him very much and will never forget him.

This group helped to make it possible for me to receive a college education. Throughout the struggle, and it was indeed a mighty struggle, they stayed the course with me.

Many of us, especially those with deprived backgrounds, need encouragement while striving for something better. The magnificent group was my pillar. They are my friends for life and I would like to thank them for helping me to become a whole person, and a good citizen.

Their kindness also had an effect on the citizens of Jonesboro. Suddenly the community that had rejected, ridiculed, and reviled me on many occasions, became very supportive. No young person from this black community had ever graduated from college. So everyone began to rally and to give me much emotional support for my undying determination to receive a college education. Thank you magnificent group and thank you Jonesboro.

OUT ON MY OWN

Since my sophomore year had taken such a toll on me both physically and mentally, I decided to take a year off to work, socialize, and to get myself in a better frame of mind. So I left for New Jersey to find employment. And I joined Clint who had moved to New Jersey from Jonesboro. Now many social issues crystallized during this period.

I had visited New Jersey several times in the past. And there were two girls I had met previously. Beverly Jordan and Emma Willis were their names. With Beverly, nothing ever got started, although I liked her very much. The cause of this failure was a lack of experience on my part, and she was also older. Beverly was quite pretty and was heavily pursued by other young men. Since I had no money to speak of, my chances were slim at best. So I just went to see her and smiled a lot.

Emma was another story. We were a great hit from the beginning. And in addition, her family liked me a great deal. He mother said, I was a great catch, since being a college student. Emma didn't require much money to entertain. So we went to the movies and on many picnics together. We began to make out a lot and I knew there was a possibility of sex. But I was a virgin without a clue how to proceed.

Well my big chance came. One day we were alone at her home making out. The situation got very heated. So at the moment she was ready, I didn't know what to do. Things seemed very awkward and the sex act was never consummated. My first sexual experience was a total disaster. And I was really embarrassed.

Our relationship from there went steadily down hill. Whenever Emma saw me, she would laugh. So I avoided her. The great things I had dreamed about, and was going to do as far as sex was concerned, just went out the window. I wondered if this was the way it would always be. But I promised myself if another opportunity arose, no one would ever laugh at me again, when it came to sex.

Now my whole being wasn't about sex. But I thought it should be a part of my development. It was as natural as eating food or drinking water. At least this is what I was told. But up to now, sex and I was a disaster area.

Socially my summer wasn't going well. Making and saving money became my top priorities. So I secured a great job at Revlon, a cosmetic plant in New Jersey. The starting salary was one hundred and fifteen dollars a week. In the middle sixties, I thought this was really great money.

But there was a big problem, racism. A white girl from Lodi New Jersey worked next to me on the assembly line. We were material handlers, and had to talk to each other. The foreman, who was also white, liked this girl. He made trips over to our assembly line about every five minutes. He saw her talking to me much of the time. We worked next to each other and were essentially making small talk or something about the job. Now I felt pretty good about the prospects for making money to finance my junior year in college.

Well a few days later, the foreman called me into his office. He explained that there wasn't enough work for me. But I surmised it was because of the white girl. So I was laid off.

It was a crushing blow to lose this job and the money that could've been saved for college. But the foreman didn't lay off the white girl. I was depressed at the whole turn of events.

Being a persistent boy, I secured another job in a handbag factory. The pay wasn't good at all. One dollar per hour was the going rate for black unskilled laborers at this factory. This was just enough to cover food, clothing, and shelter. The work was also extremely hard.

To survive, I sold handbags to my relatives and their friends. These bags were called seconds and could be bought for very little money from the factory. This helped for a while. But eventually, I had to leave this job because it wasn't economically feasible to continue.

Well I secured one more job at a food processing plant in Northern New Jersey. My salary wasn't very good because this was traditionally a low paying industry. It was a menial job, but I needed the work.

As worker passed the large bins where mince meat, jams, jellies, and cherries were stored, they would stick their fingers into these bins to get a quick taste. I was really shocked at some of the practices taking place in this food plant. After witnessing this, it was a long time before I would eat jam, jelly, or cherries. And Mince meat was never one of my favorite foods.

In the area where I worked, most of the employees were black. But there was one white woman who acted like a queen. She was about fifty years of age. To me she was pretty old. Well to a boy in his late teens, most people past twenty-five years of age seemed old. But most of the black workers in this area catered to her every whim.

She asked me to do something for her one day, and I refused. I can't remember what it was. But when I said no, she proceeded to cuss at me very loudly. So I cussed back at her. She was really shocked because black workers usually wouldn't do this, especially to a white woman.

Well she immediately went to the boss, and of course, he was white. In just a few minutes, I heard my name being shouted very loudly over the intercom system. "Alfred Turnipseed, report to my office at once." Upon reporting the boss said. "There was no work for me." And of course, I was laid off again. This white woman had gotten me fired. The boss didn't ask me for an explanation either.

So then I began to realize that education was the key to my future success. These companies had actually done me a great favor. They had shown me the way.

I called Miss Arnold and told her the story. Up to now, no money had been saved. I didn't have my fare back to Atlanta. So Miss Arnold sent it to me with no complaints or comments. I was happy she didn't scold me. But I was very embarrassed, to say the least. Well I was back where I started. But was much wiser, and with a much healthier attitude toward education.

This all happened during one summer and one semester. And I experienced many changes in this short period of time. Many of these changes helped to shape my attitude toward sex, education, and life itself. These experiences would help in my quest to become a whole person.

Miss Arnold picked me up from the airport with a smile. She probably knew these experiences were good for me, but didn't mention them at all. She made me promise to get back in school and stay there until I graduated. Well I promised. Now my formal education would continue.

Most people in the black community of Jonesboro knew why I had stayed out of school for the previous semester. It was an unsuccessful attempt to work and save money for school.

A great scholarship benefit, sponsored by members of the magnificent group was created to give support for my return to school. This was one of the most beautiful gestures that could happen to me. The whole community was involved. And this said to me. You are important, we love you, and we support you. It touched my heart to the very core. I received clothing, money for books, and tuition for the next school year.

A NEW BEGINNING

Junior year

I reentered college with much anticipation but with some trepidation as well. The extra burden from the community and their expectations were added to the mix of trying to be a success. Many social, mental, and emotional changes would take place during this year.

Before college, my parent didn't approve of card playing. Well while in New Jersey, I learned to play a variety of card games. Many college students were really into cards. And the most popular college card game at the school was Bid Whist.

My good friend Mel Tucker and I formed a team and became very good at the game of bid whist. Well we practiced enough. There were other fine players like, George Brown, Laura Foster, Mattie Jean molder, and James Sean.

These players along with Mel and I, became so skillful, a ranking system was instituted. After the ranking system, then an annual tournament was set in motion.

The team of Al Turnipseed and Mel Tucker (called T'N'T') won the tournaments for my junior and senior years. Mel was ranked number one in the system and I was number three. It was great being card champions. We probably spent too much time with this activity and not enough time with our studies.

My reputation grew as a result of this game and I was more socially accepted. I was actually having real fun for the first time in my college career. I also became really skilled at other card games during these years.

I learned social dancing during this year. But the Cha Cha, which I had learned in high school, was still my favorite. A classmate named Annette Dustee and I, were Cha Cha champions. We only danced the Cha Cha with each other and had a variety of really slick moves. The other dance teams wouldn't challenge us at all. We were really good.

While at social dances, girls would actually ask me to dance. This helped me feel better about myself because I had found something else that I could do very well.

Sure I felt better, but was still a pronounced stutterer, still had problems with self esteem, and my confidence was not what it should've been.

Since I had learned to dream, being a participant in all phases of college life was still fleeting.

Activities like, being a member of the student government, having major roles in plays, and a respected member of the chorus, were accomplishment I would never realize. So I sat on the sidelines. I became a seer but wanted to be a doer. It was very frustrating, wanting to do something, but knowing that I couldn't.

Many young black men face this same dilemma. Being stigmatized and never getting the opportunity to show their ability. I understood why people became frustrated and embarked on destructive paths. But my way of expression was different. I just had to keep fighting. And I still had a long way to go with no clear path to follow.

A speech class was mandatory for graduation. So I took a course from an instructor named Ms. Pance. But she preferred "Ponce." It was a course in which all students received an "A," if on the final examination a poem by Dylan Thomas was recited. She adored this author and his poems.

I stood up when it was my turn to recite and said absolutely nothing. She didn't know I was having stutterers freeze up. This is when no sound would come out of your mouth, although you were trying. She said. "You are going to get an F." How could I flunk a course like speech?

Later I went to her office and explained the situation. She seemed somewhat sympathetic. So I received a "C" in a course where everyone who could breathe, received an "A." And with this, I was relieved.

Now this is a great opportunity to explain my conceptions of stuttering. This is viewed from each stutterers own prospective. But we all have many traits in common. This is stuttering as it relates to me.

It is a very complex problem that will not allow me to say things I want to say when I want to say them. It is like someone suddenly putting me in a choke hold to keep the words in, so they can't be released. No matter what, the words just won't come out. There were no schools or hospitals in the South at that time, to help or treat this type of condition, especially in the black communities.

There are tricks I use. For example if making a phone call, since the person on the receiving end cannot see me, as a stutterer, I can bang my hands, stomp my feet, or jump up and down, in order to shake the words out. Going through all types of gyrations for the purpose of shaking words out, is a way of life for stutterers.

If I am out in public jumping and banging to shake words free, would be very embarrassing. People would think I was crazy. So I pinch myself, and squeeze my hands, for the express purpose of loosening the chokehold of stuttering.

The fear of authority is another problem for me. Self image and self esteem are also major issues. I try to hide from the public. So in order to survive, I live in my own world. People laugh at me all the time. This causes more fear and a farther retreat into my very small world. Stutterers deal with problems like these all the time. So this affliction is a real downer.

Will my speech ever be normal is a question stutterers are constantly asking. The answer is no, but this problem can now be dealt with. I am still dealing with this problem

In college I had a crush on a very smart girl named Teresa Wakefield. I liked her during my first two years there. But I never said anything to her other than hello and good by. Being a stutterer, I figured my chances with her were nonexistent. During a college reunion a few years ago, I mentioned this to Teresa. She was quite surprised and was under the impression I didn't like her at all. Well we both had a good laugh about this.

Academic wise, things were going well. I still had a heavy load, but this by now was the norm for me. In my fraternity, most functions were also going well.

I met a girl at the beginning of the school year named Edna freeman. She was a freshman from a small town in the southern part of Georgia called Haharia. I had never heard of this town. She said it was near Savannah Georgia. She was unsophisticated in many ways, but was quite intelligent with a refreshing personality. I also thought she was very pretty.

Her family owned a tobacco farm. And she was quite a country girl, and I liked her almost immediately. She was also a music student, so we had that in common. We began to talk to each other and things started happening. We went on dates to the movies and to concerts.

One day we found ourselves alone in the music department. We started to kiss and things got really passionate. We started to touch each other and things just went further and further. Edna told me she was a virgin. So here I was with a girl who was a virgin, and I was supposed to be "the great teacher." Actually, I was also a virgin.

The little experience I had during the past summer was of no consequence. So we felt and touched each other more and more. Now things were really out of hand. We decided to go all the way. Well we tried intercourse, but it didn't work because she felt pain. Stories had been told to me about girls becoming frigid if this process wasn't dealt with properly. I didn't know whether this was true or not, but I was determined to put her needs ahead of mine. So I was quite willing to wait and take as much time as needed. So we stopped. But we continued to date and she felt more and more comfortable with me. Whenever alone, we continued to experiment, each time going just a little further than the previous time.

By now I liked Edna a lot. And since I was the chosen one with whom she would lose her virginity, this situation had to be handled with great sensitivity. At this point in my life, I was really sensitive to the needs and feelings of inexperienced people. I was one of them.

After many experiments, we arrived. This was great. It was my first success with intercourse. Edna loved it. And she thanked me for been so patient and loving during the whole experience. This made me feel like a really good person. After our first great experience, we were intimate about once a week, then twice, and then almost every day. This was as great as I could have imagined. And we were growing much closer every day.

She was the permanent one. Things had taken a turn upward for me. I was no longer a virgin, had a girl friend, and was more fulfilled than at any point in my life.

Edna and I would go to my sister Barbara's apartment, while she was working, to be intimate. And toward the end of my junior year, I had rented a house with two other college fellows. Edna and I would go there whenever we could.

I remembered the promise made to myself after the Emma Willis disaster. No girl will laugh at my sexual prowess again. Well Edna never did. And all during our courtship, she was very patient with me and my stuttering situation.

Edna's mother didn't like me at all. She knew her daughter had lost her virginity to me. I was called by her a "city slicker." I can't imagine a boy like me being called this. Mrs. Freeman was the matriarch of the family and Edna was very close to her. Nothing happened in this family unless pre-approved by Mrs. Freeman.

In high school, when Edna went to her senior prom, the boy met her there. Mrs. Freeman took and picked her up when the prom was over. She would always tell her mother everything. Mrs. Freeman had a very strong influence on her daughter's thinking and her actions.

If she had given herself a chance to know me, she would've realized that I had her daughter's best interest at heart. And if I had been another type of person, her daughter could've easily been taken advantage of in many ways. But Mrs. Freeman thought I was just no good.

I was invited down to Edna's home toward the end of the school year. She gave me explicit instructions on how to get there.

Take the bus down past Savannah, Georgia and have the driver drop you off near the white gate on Clove Street.

Upon arriving at the prescribed point, Edna and her mother met me. We rode in silence for about a mile through tobacco fields and arrived at their home. I was pleasantly surprised because the home was very beautiful, very spacious, and very tastefully decorated.

They got me settled because I was supposed to stay the night. I had a change of clothes, another pair of shoes, and my yearbook. After settling in, we had dinner. And this was when all hell broke loose.

With Edna's virginity lost, Mrs. Freeman asked me this question, "What are your intentions?" Since I wasn't skilled in parental tactics, I answered, "My intentions are to finish school." Well that was the wrong answer. And I learned later that Mrs. Freeman was thinking about marriage for me and her daughter. Well we were certainly on different pages.

After expressing her displeasure and how she felt about me, like you are no good, just like all other boys, only after one thing, and many other choice words, she demanded that I leave. She also warned me not to be there when Mr. Freeman arrived. Now during this entire confrontation, Edna never uttered a word. Here I was about three hundred and fifty miles from home, not knowing where the hell I was, Mrs. Freeman yelling and screaming for me to leave her home, and Edna being a complete mute.

Suddenly fear overwhelmed me. I rushed to gather my belongings. Mrs. Freeman wouldn't take me to the bus area. So I rushed through the tobacco fields in mortal fear. What if I met Mr. Freeman? What would I say or do?

Fortunately, I didn't meet him before arriving at the bus stop. Now waiting for the bus filled me with tremendous anxiety. I prayed for it to arrive soon. Well finally, it did. But now, I had to flag it down. Did the driver see me? Would he stop? Well the bus stopped, and a sigh of relief gripped me. Now boarding the bus, there was a seat in the rear. What If they were following the bus? I was still filled with fear. So I stared out the back window for many miles before being able to relax.

Arriving home, I discovered the extra pair of shoes and my yearbook had been left behind. Well I wasn't going back to retrieve them or call for that matter. I was just happy to be home in one piece. Ma was surprised that I had such a short stay. And I never told her what happened on this harrowing trip.

This was the end for Edna and I. Mrs. Freeman made sure of that by keeping her out of school at Clark until I graduated. But she continued her education at Clark and graduated, after I left. I spoke with Edna on one occasion after this incident. She expressed what I already knew. Her mother hated me and forbade her to ever see me again. And Edna was not strong enough or didn't want to go against her mother's wishes.

I probably couldn't have made it with Edna anyway. She didn't have a mind of her own. But the time with her was very good. The relationship was a tremendous step in my development.

But I wouldn't want to go through this type of experience again. Edna got married a few years later, and is very happy, I was told. This pleased me very much because it turned out well for her.

Many changes had occurred during the year. I learned and grew a great deal. The sex monkey was off my back. The years of pinned up energy had been relieved. And I felt more normal. Now I could focus on other developmental issues. I had to keep my life moving forward.

The summer was filled with anxiety and anticipation. Since the coming year would be my fourth in college. Would I actually graduate?

Well Miss Arnold held my hand the entire summer and assured me that I would.

I worked with Da-Cliff most of the summer on the junk truck. In my spare time, working in Miss Arnold's garden, cutting her grass, and keeping her car clean was still a priority. Extra money was made selling copper, aluminum, Christmas trees, and doing various odds jobs. School clothes were purchased with monies earned during the summer. And for the balance of the year, things progressed normally.

Many exciting events were scheduled to take place during the next year. This was my senior year. And no one in my family had ever gone this far. They were all anticipating having a college graduate among them.

SENIOR YEAR

There were a number of things to be done as requirements for graduation. I had to write and score a musical composition. My choice was a march that turned out pretty good. The marching band played my composition at one of the football games, and it was received very well.

I had to take other courses in counterpoint and orchestration. The knowledge from these courses was needed for scoring and writing more complicated musical compositions. I passed these courses with flying colors.

Since music majors had to exhibit playing proficiency on most major instruments, I took courses in woodwinds and strings. They were quite enjoyable and I became a decent saxophone player and was not too bad on the bass fiddle. My senior year was progressing normally and without much fanfare.

Miss Arnold helped me with the purchase of a class ring and other senior expenses. The senior dance was coming up and I didn't have a date. Since Edna Freeman didn't return for my senior year, I had no girlfriend.

Experience with the opposite sex during this period, was limited to a series of friends only type dates, and not many of those. So I didn't go to the senior dance. It was far too expensive and I didn't feel that I would miss very much either.

In order to graduate, music majors had to exhibit a high level of playing proficiency on their chosen major instrument. My major instrument was the French horn.

So I began to prepare for my horn recital. I practiced a great deal over the next two weeks for this event. My program was approved by the head of the music department. So I was set and ready to go.

On the evening of the recital, I was very nervous, and didn't believe that I could go through with the performance. So taking a friends suggestion before the concert, I went down to the local liquor store and purchased a small bottle of vodka. Now approximately thirty minutes prior to my recital, I drank the whole bottle straight up. So going onto the stage, I felt no pain. My memory of this event is sort of a blur. But the concert came off without a hitch, I was told. There were no complaints, and I received an "A" in performance. This was another major huddle cleared for graduation. With the vodka doing its job, I missed most of this event. I was drunk.

Ma, Da-Cliff, Miss Arnold, and a few other friends were present at the performance. They seemed happy and proud of me. But I didn't get close to any of them for fear of detection. They gave me strange looks and asked if I was alright? I simply said that the whole event had been overwhelming. They seemed to accept this explanation. But Da-Cliff sensed something else. I believe he knew my condition, but never mentioned it to me or to Ma. He did look at me from time to time with a rye smile that said, "I know." This really endeared Da-Cliff to me even more than before. It was quite an experience. And I will never forget it, the parts I remember.

Most of my academic course work had been completed. I had actually been cleared to graduate. My grade average for four years was an unimpressive 3.0., about a "B." But considering where I came from, this was not too bad.

Now a feeling of euphoria came over me. I was for the most part, a college graduate. This was indeed a great feeling.

Graduation day came with all the traditions befitting this event. Here I was with a cap and gown, marching down the isle of Davage

Auditorium. Was I dreaming? I had to pinch myself, but not as a stutterer. But as a person receiving something thought to be essentially impossible to obtain. It was a college degree with my name on the certificate. As I marched down the isle looking around at the other graduates and parents, my feet and my body were floating. It was a very spiritual experience. I remembered how I arrived at Clark, the sessions with the counselors, the band and chorus experiences, lack of friends, no food, being laughed at, not believing I belonged, wanting to quit, and the expectation of Miss Arnold, Ma, Da-Cliff and the family, flashed though my mind while enjoying the circumstances of this event. All the pain and heartbreaks endured over the past four years, was a distant memory. I couldn't fathom this day ever coming to pass, or in my case, ending. Well I received my degree with all the pageantry and fanfare unimaginable to me or my family.

Ma and Da-Cliff were beaming. Miss Arnold was extremely pleased and very proud. The other members of the magnificent group were full of pride and now had something to brag about. We all spent the balance of this day celebrating this wonderful event. The black community in the city of Jonesboro joined in the celebration, and now had a favorite son. This is a day I will always remember and it will live in my heart forever. I had triumphed over illiteracy. Wow, this was awesome. I had made it.

POST GRADUATION

I left Clark College and went home. My life was beginning a new, or at least a new phrase of it. Everything about me and around me was new. I was home for a couple of weeks, and the honeymoon seemingly was over. The community expected me to do something. I had no job and no prospects for one. The feeling of helplessness came over me, the same as it had in high school. I was armed with a piece of paper and thrust out into the world.

In collage, Music was my major and Education was my minor. I was qualified to be a teacher. But somehow knowing I would never become one. How could I teach without being able to speak? Stuttering was still a major problem for me. But what was I to do? Depression was slowing replacing the feeling of euphoria experienced before. Somehow I just had to get away from everything.

So I left Jonesboro for New York City. Somehow and somewhere, I had to secure a place for myself in the world. If I were going to fail, it wouldn't be under the scrutinizing eyes of my family, the magnificent group, or the community of Jonesboro. Since I had no job prospects, or anything going me, this was reason enough to leave my family and the city of Jonesboro.

My sister Dot encouraged me to come to New York and move in with her. Since I knew her family very well, it was an easy transition. But there were still no job prospects.

Post Graduation

After a few months of wandering about with nothing really happening, and being homesick, I wondered if I had made a mistake by moving to New York.

I spent Christmas away from home for the first time in my life. Walking down One Hundred and Twenty Fifth Street, in New York City at Christmas, listening to the song, "Georgia on my mind," was one of the loneliest times in my life. I had no real friends, and no girlfriend was on the horizon. Life at this point, had no meaning. I wasn't getting anywhere. Dot and her family gave me all their support, but I had to get something going.

I landed a job at the Joseph P. Kennedy Community Center in New York City. Having worked at this center as a part-time employee one summer, now I was hired full time. My official title was Group Leader. I reached out into the community to help troubled children, kind of a social worker. The starting salary was five thousand dollars per year. Well I surmised that this occupation wouldn't make me wealthy, but it was a beginning. And working with kids was quite enjoyable, especially the younger ones.

At the center, the administrator asked me to start a rhythm band. Well having been a music student in college, this idea appealed to me greatly. And this was my first band directorship. So I directed, and played piano. The young children enjoyed it and things were going well. But this wasn't my idea of a great occupation. There was no money to be made, and I had living expenses.

There was a young woman named Hazel Bryant employed at Kennedy Center. She was the female equivalent to me, in terms of occupation. We developed a strong friendship and discussed many issues concerning life, including stuttering. Since my stuttering wasn't getting any better, she encouraged me to enter a speech hospital. I didn't know there were hospitals for speech impediments anywhere.

Upon entering the first speech hospital, (I went to several), I learned many things about stutterers and stuttering. None of this knowledge helped me speak better, but I certainly understood the ramifications of stuttering much better.

My stuttering problem was diagnosed as emotional. It came about as the result of a traumatic experience. My mind immediately wandered back to the play in the fifth grade, when it all started. The therapists concluded that the experience of playing this negative role, with all its negative ramifications, was the traumatic trigger that resulted in stuttering. It was a rebellion against the pain of playing this role. This was always a mystery to me. But for the next year or so, psychotherapy, group therapy, speech clinics, and breathing exercises, were apart of my routine. All of this was done while working at Kennedy center. So my life was quite busy.

Hazel Bryant was quite an inspiration to me. She was a woman beset with many health problems. But her outlook on life was always positive. So thanks to her, I was trying to better my life's situation. Hazel later died from a heart attack. And I remember her with much love. She had pointed me in the right direction.

I knew a girl named Marie Alder, having been introduced to her a year earlier by her aunt. While employed at Kennedy Center, and while going to many speech hospitals, we began to date. This relationship grew fast and strong. And she became very important in my life.

Things seemed to be getting better. Now prospects for an even better life had entered my realm of thinking. I was employed, and had a girlfriend who loved me. What could be better? At this point, I had it all. And this was very new to me, but I loved it.

For the next year, Marie and I continued to have a great relationship. We went everywhere and did everything together. My whole family had gotten to know her, because she was the one I planned to marry. It was a match made in heaven. She was warm, was a very good dancer, had a great disposition, was a snappy dresser, and had a great outlook on life.

During this period, the army was complicating my life. I had been drafted several times and deferred just as many times. So my life was kind of in a state of flux. Somehow this problem had to be solved. I had to move on with my life.

Post Graduation

So I came up with this brilliant idea, join the army and get it over with. Well this is exactly what I did. Marie in the meantime, came up with another brilliant idea, so she thought. It was, let's get married.

I was almost twenty-one years old and she was nineteen. To me, we were entirely too young. I tried to explain my position to her, but to no avail. I had no career, and was still trying to find myself. So getting married at this time, was a blueprint for failure, I lamented.

Coming up through the ranks as I had under extreme pressure, my thinking was clear and practical. Let's wait until we are older, more established, and know who we are. Marriage would then have a better chance of success. Marie wouldn't accept any of this theory and demanded marriage now, or forget any future we might have together.

With a sword in my heart, I didn't yield to this ultimatum. But I did grieve continuously for a long time. Yes, my heart was really broken. In my life, I had experienced much pain. But this was more hurtful in a different way.

I went into the army with a broken heart. It would take a really long time for me to recover from this setback. Many times I wanted to pick up the phone and tell her yes. But I didn't because it would've been the wrong decision. And down the road, we both would've regretted it.

Miss. Arnold said to me once, "some of your most important decisions will hurt the most, but you must make them." She was right as usual. So now another phase of my life had ended. But there was still a long road ahead.

THE UNITED STATES ARMY

The army was where I really started to get my life together. I volunteered just to move my life ahead. Instead of having a US serial number, I had an RA serial number. A US is a draftee and an RA is a volunteer.

The army recruits from the New York area were inducted at a federal center near Battery Park in New York City. But basic training was conducted at Fort Gordon, in Augusta Georgia, for many soldiers from the northeast.

Since I was a college graduate and probably one of the oldest soldiers in my group, the Sergeant assigned me the job of Platoon Guide. I was responsible for and in charge of all soldiers drafted or volunteered in my group.

This assignment had its privileges. There would be no guard duty, No KP (kitchen duties), and no CQ. Being a gofer and to run errands for the company commander, were the duties of the CQ. And along with this new assignment came a private room. My army career had gotten off to a wonderful start.

In basic training, I was very agile and athletic. So I just sailed through the training, except for one thing, the infiltration course.

This type of training dictates that a recruit must crawl in a trench under wire, while live rounds of ammunition are fired over his head.

So I decided this was too dangerous, and I wasn't going to do it. But the question was how do I get out of it?

Now the Sergeants have heard every excuse and knew every trick in the book. Well I used one of the old standards, I got sick. In order to convince them of my illness, I had to convince myself. Now the mind can be programmed into believing mostly anything. So I really became physically ill with the help of a little mind control. Headache, vomiting, fever, I had it all. This convinced me that I could control my own destiny while in the service. And because I was so ill, the company commander sent me to the hospital. Thus, there was no infiltration course for me.

From this point, basic training was fairly easy for me. The training staff worked on our minds, trying to get us to buckle under the pressure and to quit. This was funny to me. And since I knew what they were trying to accomplish, it had no affect on me at all.

My major problem at the time was taking shots and inoculations. I was frightened to death of those things and remain so. I was threatened with all types of punishment, but to no avail. I was just plain scared of needles. Members of the medical staff held me down, strapped me to a bed, and then gave me shots. This scene was repeated over and over during my army career. And I screamed at each encounter. When I was assigned to overseas duty, this scene was worst because there were many more powerful shot to be taken. Well I surmised all of us are afraid of something.

Fort Gordon was about three hours from Atlanta. So I visited my family often when the opportunity arose. Things were working well for me at the time.

At the end of basic training was a major physical test. It consisted of the run dodge and jump, the low crawl, the grenade throw, the high bars, and the mile run wearing combat boots. This stuff was easy for me because I was in great shape, very agile and was a tremendous athlete.

I was leading the platoon with a score of four hundred heading into the mile run. Well long distance running was never my strong suit. And I couldn't negotiate the mile run and was soundly defeated by a soldier named Saul Clay, who would later become the star center fielder for a major league baseball team. But it was a good test, and I enjoyed it very much. I was a sprinter, not a long distance runner.

Basic training was now over and most soldiers were being assigned to army posts all over the country for advanced training. My family was concerned that I might go to Vietnam.

Since my buddy worked in the company headquarters, I sneaked a peek at my assignment orders. They said Fort Polk in Louisiana. Right away I headed over to the library, to gather information about the new assignment. To my amazement, this was for jungle training. Now I knew this wasn't for me because the next duty assignment after this would be Vietnam. Well I decided I wasn't going there. Now the next question was how do I get out of this assignment?

There was a saying in the army. "Tell it to the chaplain." This simply meant, when one has a problem, the chaplain is the person most likely to help get the problem resolved. Well that's exactly what I did.

While speaking with the chaplain about my past church related experiences, like working with the Young Adult Fellowship, singing in the church choir, and working in Sunday school, we concluded that I would be of better use to the army as a Chaplains assistant. This appealed to me. Then I wouldn't go to Fort Polk.

Well the company commander refused to have my orders changed. So back to the chaplain I went. He immediately called Washington and had my orders reversed. In the military, especially the army, your talents are often misused. Well I was determined not to let this happen to me. I also noticed most of the manual labor was done by black soldiers. And white soldiers usually supervised the details. Now I wasn't going to fall into that dilemma either. After all I was a college graduate, and firmly believed that my intelligence exceeded most of the army personnel in those supervisory positions. So I learned to manipulate the army machine.

Prior to the Fort Polk incident, I was primed for Officers Candidate School. My goal was to spend at least twenty-five or thirty years in the military. But because of the Vietnam situation, I changed my mind. I have always believed if I had opted to stay in the military, and if the situation had been more favorable, I would have become and retired a General. So since I didn't become an officer and a gentleman, I had to make the best of whatever was left.

My assignment orders were changed. I was sent to Fort Dix in New Jersey and went to the Chaplains Assistantship School. Now this was good. I learned to type, to organize, and to supervise an office. These skills have always been beneficial to me.

Most of my buddies went to Fort Polk. And for me, Fort Dix was about fifty miles from my home in New York City. So up to now, I was still in control of my destiny, and this had to continue.

I endeared myself to the company commander and spent much time in New York City trying to win Marie back. Well it didn't work out. So I gave up on her for good.

But my training was going very well. And when it was over, my new assignment was in South Korea. So I spent about one month with my family in Jonesboro and in New York City. Then with many other soldiers, was flown to San Francisco for my trip to Asia.

I was quite excited about the trip to Asia. We boarded a huge ocean liner about nine hundred feet long, that had been transformed into a troop carrier. This was to be my first experience traveling so far on such a large ship. Now being prone to seasickness, I didn't look forward to it.

After leaving the California coast, I became seasick. But this was happening to most soldiers, so I was not alone. Soldiers were throwing up everywhere and very often. This trip was not exciting at all, a least up to now. Imagine going to sleep looking at water, and awaking up looking at water.

Seasickness is one miserable feeling and I stayed sick for days. But during the trip, normal activities took place. We slept, ate, played cards, read, and kept the ship clean.

One day after waking up and eating breakfast, a tall green strip of land was spotted rising from the ocean floor to the sky. It was Diamond Head in Hawaii and the ship docked there. This was the most beautiful place I had ever seen in my entire life. It was green and lush and the natives had golden brown skin. This was paradise to a small town boy from Jonesboro Georgia.

Since we had been cooped up in the ship for so long, most soldiers headed for Hotel Street after we arrived. This was the place you went to get laid. But I went in the opposite direction. My idea was to see some of the cultural aspect of Hawaii, to take in the beauty, and to see how the natives lived. Well I never got laid there. But had a very rewarding stay and saw sights so beautiful, I will never forget them.

Our stay in Hawaii came to an abrupt end. It was far too short. So now we boarded the ship again and continued our trip to Korea. As we sailed further into Asia, I became seasick again.

Many days passed as we sailed through the Philippine Islands. Even with the bouts of seasickness, I actually started to enjoy the adventure.

We arrived in Korea. The ship anchored in Pusan, the southernmost coast of South Korea. Now Troops were bussed to compounds and posts all over this tiny nation. I was assigned to an artillery company.

Arriving at my post, I noticed many dowdy and dreary looking women lurking nearby. Well I suppose this was the ritual that went on from time to time when there were new arrivals. These women were looking over the new blood, a source of their income for the next year.

They were called businesswomen, not prostitutes, as we would commonly refer to women who sold their bodies. Many of the women supported entire families, I would learn later. And they would become angry if referred to as prostitutes.

After seeing these women, I swore that I would never go into the village to get laid. Well after about two weeks, my hormones were getting the better of me, and off to the village I went. And to my amazement, those dowdy looking women began to look pretty good.

Some were very attractive, especially after they were dressed properly and with makeup. Things were looking and going great.

I was assigned a Jeep to chauffeur the chaplain on his many trips to the various military posts. As a Chaplains assistant, I was assigned a chapel. And in addition, a soldier in the South Korean Army was assigned to be my assistant. This was just great. So being a Chaplains Assistant wasn't too bad.

I actually ran the chapel. In doing so, I met many interesting people. Some were Koreans, and some were Japanese. But all had musical interest. Since I had studied music, this was really great for me.

I was invited to a Korean wedding for a couple met one Sunday in the chapel. Friends invited me to visit Young Se University and Iwa University for women, (the Radcliff of South Korea). As a result of my position, I had great status.

My accommodations were also very good. I had a private room. Other soldier lived in the barracks. My clothing was kept cleaned and pressed by my assistant. This was indeed a position of prestige and I loved it. The chaplain relied on me a great deal and was very pleased with my work. I knew how to greet people and make them feel comfortable. The chapel was always tastefully decorated with flowers cut daily. The chaplain seemed to be very pleased with my handling of the chapel.

I was sent on very important and sensitive missions for the religious community of the various military posts. My assistant was also very accomplished in religious matters. I was very important and knew it. As company Chaplains Assistant, I was exempt from all extra military duties. Wow, I had it made.

Since this was essentially a laid back position, my stuttering problem was not a major stumbling block. Other nationalities seemed to be more tolerant of my problem.

By this time, going to the village to get laid, had become a regular routine. But the company commander and the chaplain got wind of it and I was warned. "Stay out of the village, especially with my Jeep," said the chaplain.

His Jeep had a huge religious cross attached to the front grill. Since the chaplain was an officer, he had to be saluted. Soldiers would naturally salute the Jeep whenever they saw it. Sometimes it would be me in the village and not the chaplain.

The company commander threatened to send me up to the demilitarized zone, if I was sighted in the village again. Well I was a regular soldier, not the chaplain. And how was I going to stay out of the village? Since I was relatively new at getting laid, this was becoming one of my great pleasures.

But up on the demilitarized zone, soldiers were constantly getting shot. This zone was the boarder between North and South Korea. It was definitely not a place I wanted to go. But I knew sooner or later, someone would see me, and report it to the chaplain or company commander. And it would be over for me.

Since I wasn't going to stand still for this to happen, a way out of this dilemma had to be found. But under no circumstances was I going to let the army decide my fate.

Having a musical background, I secretly auditioned for a touring soldiers group that entertained military personnel all over the Far East. This was done without the permission of the company commander, the chaplain, or the first sergeant.

In the military, there is a chain of command and it is strictly adhered to. I bucked the entire system by taking it upon myself to secretly audition. But I passed the audition, and just waited for new orders to be issued assigning me to this group. Now during the brief waiting period, the audition was not mentioned to the company commander or anyone in the chain of command.

So when the new orders were issued and received by me, I took them to the first sergeant and the company commander for implementation. They both flew into a rage, calling me all sorts of names and using many four-letter words. They knew I had challenged the system and won. They knew I had defeated them. There would be no demilitarized zone duty for me. I listened to them rant and rage, but my orders were clear. I was still in control of my destiny. I was smarter than they were, so I believed.

Never having guard duty or performing various other military duties, I couldn't fathom doing that ridiculous army stuff. Since entering the military, I had been exempt from all extra duties. But under no circumstances was I a dud or a fuck up as a soldier.

A day or two later, the first sergeant threw my equipment and clothing, from my room out onto the ground. I suppose this was his last act of frustration before implementing my orders. A military vehicle was sent to transport me to my new unit.

But I really enjoyed the stint as a Chaplains Assistant. Exploring the world of tanks and armed military vehicles, my Jeep, my assistant (kim), bivouacking in various areas of South Korea, meeting new friends, and my development as a person, were some of the many things that made this period special in my life. I will never forget it.

The First Cavalry Chorus, later The Second Division Showmen was my next assignment. Now my time in the army, while stationed in South Korea, became just a pleasure. Assuming my new duties was met with much enthusiasm. The new group was a traveling entertainment troupe. We rehearsed in the mornings and performed in the evenings. Our duties were to entertain military personnel from all over the Far East. This was great stuff. There were about thirty soldiers in this troupe. And they were some of the most talented entertainers I had ever met.

We traveled to Japan, Okinawa, Guam, Hawaii, and of course South Korea. We also appeared on armed forces radio and television. Accommodations for us were first class. Our uniforms were tailor made. And we had many different types. Living quarters for us, came with a houseboy to do all chores.

I had a pass to go out into the village every day. We enjoyed the best food and alcohol, (for those who drank). At that time I didn't drink, but did party a great deal.

No one bothered us because we were privileged people who brought joy to soldiers a long way from home. This was indeed an awesome responsibility. But we performed magnificently night after night to packed audiences. They really loved us.

In addition to this, I conducted several musical groups among friend cultivated while a Chaplain's Assistant. I was having the time of my life.

The First Cavalry Chorus performed with Mary Martin and Helen Hayes among others, in the Far East. This was especially good, because these entertainers had in their troupes, many young females looking for fun. My life was looking better all the time because much of the dreariness in it had disappeared.

About this time, my major problem of stuttering was beginning to be less and less important. Entertaining every night, I had a chance to look and listen to a lot of soldiers. And they had problems sometimes much greater than my own. So by focusing on other things, I stuttered less. But the problem hadn't disappeared and would never disappear. But being able to step away, to refocus, and to realize there were other problems in the world, and other people had them, gave me the assurance that I was not the only imperfect being God had created. Things certainly looked better in many respects.

By now the soldiers in my group were very comfortable with their surroundings. Most went to the village everyday to get laid. But it carried an awesome responsibility in this way.

There were diseases the medical establishment hadn't heard of. Upon entering this country, a film was shown to all soldiers concerning venereal diseases. This film was so graphic, it scared me to death and I never forgot it. So I never took chances. Whenever a soldier went to the village, the first sergeant would hand him a condom. The message was clear, never take a chance. This was also true of the food and water. I never took a chance on any of this.

In addition to the businesswomen, I met a number of very warm and beautiful South Koreans who were not in the business (selling themselves). One was named Young Sil Chun. I liked her very much and she liked me. We became very good platonic friends. Young Sil was a music student with a voice like a nightingale. I would've liked to work with her more extensively, but had to leave Korea for the USA before this could be done.

She later came to the USA, married a very nice Korean minister, and invited me to the wedding. After this, I lost contact with her. But she was a very good friend.

I taught another young Korean woman a Christmas carol. She was so happy that I was introduced to her brother. In Korea, for an American soldier to be introduced to a relative, was a sign of great respect.

In South Korea, most people in this country were poor. Well this young woman, named Miss Pak, gave me the most beautiful handkerchief one can imagine. It made me very happy because I knew it was very difficult to obtain this gift. I lost contact with her also. But these are some experiences that touched my life, while in South Korea

Another interesting experience happened during the Christmas Holidays in South Korea. We had to perform for soldiers up on the demilitarized zone. Yes, I finally made it there. This is where South Korea ends and North Korea begins. There were no gates or fences to separate the two, only minefields.

Imagine singing Christmas carols across this zone. I was in fear of my life because soldiers on both sides were often shot or assaulted. Well no one was injured, but I was happy when it was over.

We traveled to Japan. And this was another very rewarding experience. Visiting Hiroshima was the trip of a lifetime. We were at ground zero where the Atomic Bomb was dropped on Japan. Some older Japanese were still very angry at the American military. Aside from that, it was a beautiful country, and the food was exceptionally good.

Throughout the balance of my tour in the Far East, I can state it was the most interesting, rewarding, educational, and fun time of my life. From the trains rides all over South Korea, planes rides to Japan, trips to Hawaii visiting the Pearl Harbor Memorial of entombed soldiers, performing in Guam, performing on television, and meeting some of the world's great people, this period had to rank among the most fulfilling in my life.

It gave me a chance to mature and grow up. I learned to survive away from my family. Since I could focus on other things, my stuttering had dissipated, well somewhat. Emotionally, I was in a much better place. But all good things must come to an end. My tour of duty was ending in the Far East and I had to return to the USA.

In my mind, I was comparing Jonesboro to South Korea. Jonesboro was a sleepy little town. The people were poor and segregation was the rule of the day. And this wasn't a very worldly city. Korea was also very poor at that time, but with a class system. The people were very warm and friendly. They were also generally more aware of the world's situation. Maybe the war spotlighted this. Their culture was quite different. And their clothing was very colorful. As a young man from the small town of Jonesboro, this experience was priceless. It enhanced me educationally and culturally.

But in addition to saying goodbye to the many new friends acquired during this period, there were other duties I had to perform. The tailor made uniforms had to be returned along with the extra clothing assigned to me. Any extra equipment also had to be returned, and I had plenty.

But the most important business was to get my shot and inoculations record in order. Without this, reentry into the USA was impossible.

Also prior to leaving and since I had more time remaining in military service, selecting an Army posts in the USA for my new assignment, was the next order of business. I presented three choices

Now this didn't mean I would receive either. But Fort Hamilton in New York was my first choice, Fort Monmouth in New Jersey was second, and Fort Dix in New Jersey was third. Well my new assignment was Fort Monmouth in New Jersey. This was about fifty miles from my home in New York. I was still in control of my destiny.

On the day of embarkation, I boarded a plane to America. And I must say it was a great relief to take a plane and not a troop ship.

I presented my orders and my shot record to the officer of the day just prior to boarding the plane. Then I boarded without the necessary shots to do so. The officer carefully examined my shot record and ordered two MPs (military police) to remove me from the plane.

I was escorted to a very small room where doctors waited to administer all inoculations. Well screaming and yelling didn't help at all. And needless to say, this was a painful experience. Yes, there were many soldiers going through the same thing. But at least I was allowed to secure my boarding pass for my trip home to America.

My self esteem was higher, my outlook was more up beat, and my stuttering was not as severe. But there was much work to be done before I was ready to take my rightful place in this society and become a productive citizen.

ARMY, STATESIDE

I arrived in the USA with no fanfare. No horns were blowing and no banners were flying high. But what could I expect since my rank was still a PFC (private first class).

I spent my leave time between Atlanta and New York. My parents had moved into the City of Atlanta. So being with them was a lot of fun. They were happy to see me and were very proud that I could finally speak with a bit of clarity.

After relaxing and reminiscing about the previous year, I started my new assignment at Fort Monmouth in New Jersey. This assignment would prove to be the most pivotal and would have the greatest impact on my life.

I settled into my new job as company clerk for Headquarters Company at Fort Monmouth. I typed orders for soldiers receiving new assignments. In many instances, I had an impact on where those assignments would be. Therefore most of the personnel in my company had high regards for me. Well since I was a pretty regular guy who took his job seriously, and who did it very well, the company commander also liked me very much.

Much time was spent in New York City. I left the post on Thursday evening and returned on Monday evening. Regular weekend passes were issued from Friday evening to Sunday evening. Well I was different because the company commander was my friend.

But I was a PFC with about seventeen months of active duty left and with no real MOS or job description. The military would often put one into a position where promotions were impossible. A slot for a particular job in ones field or MOS was needed in order to receive a promotion.

Well I wanted a promotion and was determined to get one. I remembered, "Tell it to the chaplain." Yes and again, I did just that. We agreed that it was unfair for me not to be promoted with so much time left on active duty. I also reminded him that I was trained as a Chaplains' Assistant. He was impressed with this very much. So the chaplain talked to the company commander, who was also a friend of mine. Well they devised a plan for promotion to E4.

A slot for mail clerk was open and I was to fill this position. But in essence, I would continue my job as company clerk. We had a mail clerk already, who probably had another title. Well this was the way the army operated during my military service. I was now an E4 and it felt pretty good. And I still had well over a year left in the service.

I worked approximately four days a week typing orders for the company commander. Therefore a lot of my time was spent playing cards with the Caucasian soldiers, not the Black soldiers.

I didn't like to lose at cards and was not a very good gambler either. Black soldiers took card playing very seriously. This was especially true with games of chance (gambling). Most White soldiers didn't take it as seriously. So I chose to play with the white soldiers. They came to lose money, and I came to win.

When payday came at the beginning of the month, the white soldiers owed me lots of money and I loved it. This enabled me to purchase a lot of stereo equipment, cameras, clothing, and other items.

I became friends with a Philadelphian named Bob Guess, the company's supply sergeant. Most military people always advised me, if you are going to befriend anybody, make sure the company's cook and the supply sergeant are included. Bob Guess, the supply sergeant, became my best friend, and the company's cook always owed me money. Therefore I received extra rations and Bob supplied me with everything in the way of extra equipment like boots, clothing, coats, and tools. I was in charge, and this was really great.

Since his last name was Guess, and mine was Turnipseed, we had lots of fun when meeting strangers. They would ask me my name, and I would say, "Turnipseed." After asking several times and being perplexed, they would then turn to Bob and ask, "Well what is your name?" Bob would say, "Guess." They would reply, "I cannot guess, so just tell me." Bob would again say, "Guess." This banter went back and forth until Bob and I produced identification cards. This was very funny and we really milked it.

I could always count on Bob, no matter what the odds were. If there were fifty guys waiting to beat me up, Bob would stand by my side. He looked after me like a big brother.

For instance, one day a white soldier called me a "Nigger." I didn't have to touch the guy. Bob beat him up, threw him down a flight of stairs, and made him apologize to me.

After this incident, nobody bothered me, because they didn't want to deal with Bob. He was a really big guy and was a really good friend. I miss him very much.

Most of my military career had been spent in the entertainment area. And I desperately craved this again. But very little was provided because of New York and Atlantic City being so close by. The soldiers could provide their own entertainment. So I had to find something else to stimulate me.

The post had a football team, and a very high level one at that. So I set my sights on joining. I always believed that I had the ability to play for any college team in the country. And on the post team were players from major colleges and universities all over the country. This would be a great challenge.

I began a vigorous exercise and weight training program. It went very well because I built my body into a finely turned athletic machine of about one hundred and seventy five pounds. Training camp for prospective members also worked out well. Not only did I make the team, I became a starter. Then I was touted as the teams' star player. Fans flocked to the games to see me play.

My jersey number was plastered all over the sport pages of the army newspapers throughout the tri-state area. I was beginning to live a dream, and was receiving much acclaim from people living in and around the army post.

From as far back as I could remember, star athletes had the most and the prettiest girls. Well this was my chance for attention. It felt very good. And I wasn't about to let this chance escape me.

But many other great things were also happening. I didn't have to focus on my main problem of stuttering. It had dissipated to an even greater degree than before. For the first time in my life, I had prominence and notoriety. My confidence was steadily on the rise. Also for the first time in my life, I actually began to like myself. The negative and cruel things bestowed upon me in my younger days, the non-positive things I had believed all my life, were not true. I was a good person with something to contribute.

Had the veil been lifted? Had the change sort for so long, finally come? Well at this point I didn't know, but something wonderful and exciting was happening. Suddenly the world as I had known it was quite different. My friends wondered what had happened to me. Well I felt like an eagle, able to fly over everyone and everything. Wow, this was exciting.

Then I concocted philosophies about the game of football to help me succeed even more. A diagram of the field was etched in my mind. So being at point A or B in as fewer seconds as possible enabled me to gain valuable yardage.

I surmised if I ran the football twenty times a game, the opponents would stop me fifteen times. But I was going to get away at least five times. This strong belief was also etched in my heart.

In one game, I was knocked nearly unconscious. But I ran a touchdown for sixty-five yards. I didn't remember it very well, so I read the sport pages of the morning newspaper. My picture with all circumstances and details were all over the sport pages. So it did happen.

In a few games, I ran the ball down to the one-yard line. Then on the next play, the ball was given to another running back by the quarterback. He scored the touchdown, got the glory, and I had done the hard work.

So I decided never to be stopped on the one-yard line again. The only way to stop me was to kill me. So I decided to die. Then I was free to play the way I wanted to, with reckless abandon. With this new philosophy in my head, I was never stopped on the one-yard line again. Now my belief was I could accomplish anything on the football field. I was like Alexander the Great, a conqueror who could soar above everyone.

This was really great for me at this time in my life. These football experiences had become spiritual in nature. And in this football setting, I was an angel. There was a definite change taking place in my life.

By now my stuttering, although still there, was not a major factor in my new life as a football star. My confidence soared. I loved who I had become, and certainly believed the rebirth had taken place.

Now though all this new prominence, I had remained very humble. But one day I lost my focus. I was trying to impress three new girl friends. So I asked them to come to the game and see me play. I also promised to score three touchdowns, one for each of them.

So during the game, I was having my way as usual. So at a point I had scored two touchdowns, but had promised three. I had a slight injury and was not in the game at all.

I gazed across the football field at my three new friends. They waved at me. Then I knew what I had to do. Maybe just a few more carries of the football, and I would score the third touchdown. The promise of three would've been fulfilled.

The injury was nothing new to me because I had been injured before, and ran a sixty-five yard touchdown. No big deal, so back into the game I went.

On the first carry after reentering the game, I was hit with a crushing blow and was severely injured. My knee was sprained and my leg was broken. This was quite a shock and it took a few moments to comprehend what had happened.

Then I cast my eyes up to the Heavens. I asked God "was it over?" Was this the end of my reign? Would I revert back to just being an ordinary person? I remember thinking that I was a conqueror. And on the football field, I could do anything.

Now the world was spinning around me. I was confused and wasn't sure what would happen next. Well I was taken to the hospital in a state of shock.

My teammates visited me after the game. We won, and they wanted to bring me the good news. During the stay in the hospital, my three friends didn't visit me at all. And I never saw or heard from them again.

That day on the football field, I learned the lesson of my life. Never assume that you are too big for adversity to strike. God showed me that he was still in charge. Life and good fortune can be taken away with the blink of an eye. After relaying these events to Ma she said, "You had gotten too big for your britches." Well in retrospect, she was probably right. And I never forgot the valuable lessen learned this special evening while playing football.

Now I was very depressed. My life seemingly ascending had suddenly descended very quickly. Confusion had overwhelmed me and I didn't know where to turn. So I prayed, "God please help me for I am lost again."

A few days later, the company commander visited me. I was still in the hospital. So my first thoughts were he just wanted to wish me well and give me a report on the team's progress. But he had something else in mind. My life was about to undergo a major transformation. This would set the tone for my triumph over a life filled with hopelessness. God had been listening to me. He had heard my supplication.

The company commander asked me to coach the team. The current coach was being reassigned and he thought I would be perfect for the job. I couldn't believe my ears. Many of the current players were much older and I had no coaching experience. But the company commander stood fast on this recommendation.

Me a coach, I carried too much baggage. I stuttered, and I had never motivated anyone in my whole life. Also in the past, I had never communicated with any large group of people. I had fought tooth and nail just to keep my own life afloat. And I had lived in a cocoon for most of my life. So how could I coach anybody?

Again, the company commander stated that he wanted me for the job and stood firmly on his recommendation. After thinking more about it and for some reasons unknown to me, I was compelled to accept the job. There were no other plans on the horizon anyway. Although the company commander was my friend and knew of my many struggles, he showed great faith in my ability to handle a very difficult situation.

After recovering sufficiently enough from my injuries to go out on the practice field and address the football team, a huge problem arose. What happens now? What could I say? What would I do? Well since there were no immediate answers, I fired the entire team. This got everyone's attention. And I left the practice field immediately. I still don't know why the act of firing the whole team occurred.

But during the next few days, I attached a note to the bulletin board, asking men who were interested in football, to come down to the practice field and tryout for the team.

Suppose no one had showed up? My whole situation would've been very different. But since they did show up, this began one of the most satisfying periods of my life. Bits and pieces of philosophies hung onto during my playing days, became an integral part of my coaching methodology. I began to work with the team and it began to respond.

I discovered this uncanny ability to look into a player's mind, heart, and soul, and extract winning and competitive ingredients he didn't think were there. Well maybe I learned this from Miss Arnold. I was also keenly interested in the player's spirit. Watching his physical movements, at the same time looking into his eyes, gave me a wealth of knowledge as to his ability. This was a gift and a source I tapped into on many occasions.

Once during a game the defensive team was playing very poorly. So I took them out and put the offensive team on defense. This worked like a charm, and from this point, every move I made was pure magic. The players embraced my philosophy. And things were going great. For instance, some of my favorite lines went like this. "We are fighting for our lives, in essence fighting a war. The other team is playing a game of football. How can a team playing a game of football defeat a team fighting a war or fighting for its very existence?" "Therefore they have no chance." Other sayings went like this, "Never provoke the other team. Why make supermen out of mortal beings."

"Act meek and mild and the other team will relax. At that point, you hit them with all the fury that hell can muster. They will be at your mercy for the rest of the game."

I learned this from watching the Great Jimmy Brown of the Cleveland Browns play football. But my most favorite saying went like this. "Two players with the same ability and the same physical talent, but one makes All-American and one doesn't. What is the difference?" To me, the difference is the bigness of the heart and the mental capability to understand this concept. Simply stated, it is called determination.

While playing football, I was determined that my heart would be bigger than my opponents or I would die trying. This gave me the edge and I would be in control. This is what I imparted to the team. This was my commitment and the team embraced it with vigor.

Coaches must become actors at some point. Well I employed a bit of theatrics also. One game we were losing very badly. So at halftime, the team assembled in the locker room. They waited patiently for me the coach, to impart some pearls of wisdom to get them out of their playing funk. But I sat down in front of the team and began to quietly shed tears. The team sat startled and bewildered while watching me. I didn't speak during this whole episode. Imagine the effect on a team, watching its coach cry for about twenty minutes.

After halftime, the team went back onto the field and destroyed the opposing team. I smiled because my theatrics had the desired effect. I had motivated them.

There was another game we were losing badly. So at halftime, my team assembled in the locker room for me to read them the riot act. It was time for more theatrics. But I couldn't use the previous tactic because the team would think they were being hustled. It had to be something original. So I took a helmet and flung it against the cement wall. With aloud bang it shattered, and I sat staring at it in disbelief. The team watched attentively as I slowly picked up the helmet and embraced it. Not a word was spoken as I held this helmet as if it was the most precious material on earth.

Well when the halftime was over, pure magic came from my team. I smiled again, because I had touched the very soul of this team and they had touched me with their play. These tactics were theatrical, but they were also metaphorical and reached the very depth of the team's physic for the desired result. My heart was filled with love and pride for this team as we continued the season.

By this time into the season, my injuries had healed. I pondered whether to play again. But eventually, decided against it. I needed the therapy of coaching. This team and the philosophy connected with it were indeed therapeutic for me. The chemistry of this team, and what I had built, was too important to tear apart by inserting myself into the line up. I viewed this as a test, and the greater good would be accomplished by me staying the coach.

My team upset an opposing team every week on the way to the championship game. We weren't favored in any game, but we won. In the championship game, we played a team who had just steam rolled over every opponent it faced. We were supposed to lose by fifty points. Well I was not going to be a party to any massacre, especially my own.

Since they were much larger and faster than we were, I went through special preparations for getting my team mentally ready. My philosophy was this. Who cares about size because they still must block and tackle us, and this depends on execution. With our great conditioning, we will execute, block, tackle, and defend until we die. I needed to hear myself say this. My soul and psyche needed it.

My team fought and slugged with this team for the whole game. But we finally lost thirteen to six in one of the epic battles of the whole season. This was a really great game. We played like a team possessed. And when it was over, my team along with myself received a standing ovation. But they had won and they were a great team. But my team performed up and above all expectations except mine. I was extremely proud of those young men and the effort they had given. It was beautiful to see what happened to this group of men who I could motivate and inspire.

This changed my life completely. If I could motivate and inspire this group of people, then maybe I could inspire myself and succeed as a private citizen. So from this point, I believed the change had taken place. But the rebirth was continuing.

During this period of rebirth, I became very friendly with a young woman named Juanita Farmer. She had been my pen pal all during the time I was in the Far East. I wrote her many letters describing the many places visited during this period. I was very happy to have her as a pen pal. But now the relationship has become very serious and this pleased me very much.

I had finally found some one to share my life because we were married shortly before I was separated from military service. She gave me much support and would prove to be an asset in the future.

My life had taken another turn for the better. Many of the long weekends taken during the latter part of my army career, were spent with Juanita. She was very pretty, smart and was crazy about me. I always had a great time with her because of our common interest. So at this point, I couldn't ask for a better person.

I had about six months left on active duty and I wanted a promotion. My life was different because I now had a wife to support. So getting a promotion and a raise was doubly important to me.

But this time I didn't go to the chaplain. My good friend was the company commander, so I asked him about it. We decided it would be unfair not to receive another promotion. But he had to find a slot for this to happen.

The slot of duty sergeant was open. His responsibilities were to train, drill, and generally harass new recruits. Well I wasn't about that, but the commander inserted me into this slot. I was promoted to a sergeant E5. I did the same job as before, but now I wore three stripes. My final military rank would be that of a sergeant. Since military records are forever, I will be a sergeant until the day I die.

My army career was almost complete with no regrets. I had grown tremendously and will always cherish my military days. Before separating from the military, the company commander is required to give each soldier a reenlistment talk. If considering staying in the military, this was the time to make it known.

Now my good buddy, the company commander, knew I wasn't considering reenlistment at all.

But during this meeting he asked this question, "What would it take to persuade you to reenlist?" I quickly replied, "Make me a General and I will gladly reenlist." This statement ended the meeting.

But the next day I was called to his office. He gave me two General Stars. We both had a good laugh about this whole episode. I appreciated his effort, and I still have those stars and cherish them more and more each day. I separated from the military without much fanfare. In fact, there was no fanfare. But I was ready to start my life with an even chance for success. I suppose this was all I could ask. Now I was ready for the next challenge.

TRIUMPH

The coaching experience taught me many things. First, I could compete with the best and hold my own. Secondly, I had the knowledge and the skills to contribute. Thirdly, with my determination and desire, I could make a change for the betterment of my life and for others.

I had communication problems for most of my life. And also, a great deal of my life had been lived in a cocoon. But the irony of this was my lifetime occupation would be in verbal communication.

I believed the metamorphosis had taken place. And I had come full circle. From a little boy who stuttered, to a high school lad who had no confidence, to a college student who was hopelessly in over his head, to a post graduate with no place to turn, to a soldier who grew into a man, then into a contributor and a motivator, who made a difference.

I had triumphed over indifference.

I had triumphed over non-existence.

I had triumphed over despair.

I had triumphed over failure.

I had triumphed over poverty.

I had triumphed over illiteracy and ignorance.

I had triumphed over evil forces that sought to keep me from success.

I had triumphed over my own uncertainty and lack of confidence.

I had triumphed in spite of my humble beginning.

I had triumphed because of my humble beginning.

I had triumphed in spite of myself.

I had triumphed because of myself.

This was a very long, hard, tedious, and uncertain journey. But I always believed the change would occur. Now I was ready to take my place in this society among other positive influences.

I was now a complete person. I was always a good person. But now I knew it. God had heard me. And he had answered my twenty year prayer.

EPILOGUE

A few years after I had graduated and finished my military duties, this idea popped into my mind. I wanted to publicly thank the Magnificent Group for their support during my college years. Since they were all alive at the time, I wanted to give them flowers while they could smell them.

Well I called the minister of Andrews Chapel Methodist, the church I grew up in, to convey this idea to him. I would be the morning speaker for the church service, thereby thanking these seven people publicly. The minister thought this was a very good idea. So I prepared a speech called "In Honor of Love and Friendship." This speech was delivered during the morning service in June of 1976 at Andrew Chapel Church. This was the first time I had spoken publicly since the fifth grade, when I began to stutter.

Although I was afraid, some power greater than my own, compelled me to do this. This event went extremely well and the seven people were very happy.

After the speech, I presented each of the seven with plaques inscribed with these words, ("In honor of love and friendship.") This made me feel very proud and happy. The group was very proud. And Jonesboro was very proud. I will always cherish this day. It was a crowning victory for me.

Printed in the United States
141540LV00001B/6/P